GUITAR DREAMS

THE ART & ARTISTRY OF MASTER PLAYERS AND BUILDERS

Andy Volk

Cover, Graphic Design & Layout: Andy Volk
Production: Ron Middlebrook
Text © 2014, 2021 Andy Volk

ISBN 978-1-57424-406-9

Published by CENTERSTREAM Publications, P.O. Box 17878 Anaheim Hills, CA 92807
Web: centerstream-usa.com Email: centerstrm@aol.com Phone: (714) 779 - 9390

INTRO

My fingers caress the nylon strings of a classical guitar to coax forth a sultry Bossa Nova. On a different day, clanging steel string dissonances ring deliciously as *Banish Misfortune* becomes *Old Joe Clark* which eventually morphs into *Haste to the Wedding*. Later, my ear craves that ever-mysterious blend of wood, metal and air that compels me to pick up my resophonic guitar. An hour, a day, or perhaps a month later, the only prescription for what I've got is Telecaster® twang. Three Barney Kessel and two Jerry Byrd records later, I'm searching for jazz licks on a C6th lap steel.

Okay, I admit it; I cast a wide net when it comes to the guitar and other string instruments. Whether standard guitar in all its genres, electric or acoustic lap-style playing, ukulele, old-time banjo, mandolin - I love it all. In fact, I've been *compelled* to seek out the players, instrument histories, and the arcane and sometimes mysterious stories about the people who play, create and love these instruments.

Over the last few years, I've written many music arrangements and books and contributed musician and luthier profiles, interviews, and record reviews to *Acoustic Guitar Magazine, The Fretboard Journal, The Steel Guitar Forum, The Squareneck Journal* and other websites. My sincere thanks to Teja Gerkin at AG and to Michael Simmons and Jason Verlinde at FJ for their editorial guidance and passion for string instruments. Their changes invariably made my writing better.

DEDICATION

This book is dedicated to my late friend, John McGann. John was one of the finest instrumentalists I've ever heard; a musician of vast depth and a person of uncommon humor, humility and kindness. I'll never come anywhere close to his level of musicianship but whenever we jammed together, John always made me feel like I was holding my own.

CONTENTS

Muriel Anderson	7
George Barnes	17
Gino Bordin	29
Jerry Byrd	33
Cindy Cashdollar	35
Amos Garrett	39
Ben Harper	45
Bud Isaacs	55
Ray Jackson	59
Nato Lima	65
Tony Mottola	73
Joaquin Murphey	75
Skip Pitts	81
Elliott Randall	85
Louie Shelton	89
Johnny Smith	93
Gabor Szabo	101
Bill Tapia	105
Eric Weissberg	109
Rick Aiello	115
Bill Asher	126
Carroll Benoit	140
Estaban Bojourquez	149
Super Chikan	152
Bill Hardin	156
Steve Spodaryk	164
Tiki Bar Guitar	173
Photo Credits	177
Acknowledgements	178

MURIEL ANDERSON

Muriel Anderson *stops* the show. No question about it. A petite woman cradling a nylon string acoustic guitar has somehow morphed into an entire bluegrass band before our eyes and ears. Starting with a credible guitaristic imitation of clawhammer banjo, Anderson flashes a ninety watt smile as she announces each new instrument: "That leaves my thumb free so I'm going to play the bass line now. The index finger is the mandolin." As *Old Joe Clark* segues to *Foggy Mountain Breakdown* the audience erupts in laughter and applause, thrilled to have witnessed a uniquely cool feat of musical legerdemain. Shoulders sag in relaxed contemplation as Anderson follows the barn burner with an exquisite raindrops-on-flower-petals rendition of Sakura, a Japanese folk melody. Anderson is nothing if not versatile.

The first woman to win "Winfield," the National Fingerstyle Guitar Championship (held in Winfield, Kansas each year), Muriel Anderson is one of the world's most in-demand players and teachers on the acoustic scene. With a dizzying schedule of composing, master classes and international touring, she's amazed audiences for twenty years with her technical command of the instrument while charming them with the subtle beauty, bubbling humor and warmth of her music. In addition to her eight performance CDs, Anderson has recorded instructional DVDs and guitar books published by Hal Leonard, Mel Bay, and Zen-On Japan. Her music can also be heard in Woody Allen's 2008 film "Vicky Cristina Barcelona."

§

Walking around Nashville's Radnor Lake, I ask Muriel about her earliest experiences with music. She laughs, recalling that her first song was composed in response to hearing the doorbell ring. She remembers running to the piano, finding the notes, harmonizing them, and then adding lyrics; by the way, she was in kindergarten at the time.

"My sister Marguerite and I grew up without a TV until about 3rd or 4th grade. I'm sure that helped us to develop a long attention span and a fascination with how things work, which was helpful when I started playing music. "We had an old Victrola and my sister and I would clear the living room furniture out and dance," she recalls. "When I got my first guitar I remember going outside and listening to the crickets, trying to imitate their sound on the strings and play along with them."

Anderson's musical genes go back two generations to her grandfather, Andrew Jacobson, who played alto saxophone in John Phillip Sousa's band. "My grandfather was the youngest member of Sousa's band at the time.

I didn't know him very well because he died when I was young, but he was an inspiration because I thought playing music for a living was the coolest thing anyone could do." Her mother played piano and taught students in their home for many years. This early exposure culminated years later with Anderson's contest-winning arrangement of the ragtime piano classic *Nola*, a favorite of her mom's.

Anderson started guitar lessons in grade school with Anne Jones at the Jones school of Folk Music in Lombard, Illinois, joining a children's bluegrass ensemble as she progressed on the instrument. "My parents got me a Doc Watson record for Christmas – it was *Doc Watson in Nashville* - and once I put it on the turntable it just never left. I played it over and over again and used to run home from school and try to figure out what he was doing. I learned every song on that record. "I always found playing the guitar fun," she says. "It was like solving a puzzle to figure out how to get the feeling I wanted, the sound I wanted; how to get my fingers to do what I wanted them to do. A lot of it is just keeping the joy alive so it doesn't *feel* like I practiced a lot. I resisted reading music. I didn't start reading music until they made me read it in college," she says with a laugh. "I just learned by ear and chord diagrams."

Anderson enrolled as a classical guitar major at Illinois' DePaul University but hedged her bets at first with an apprenticeship in piano tuning in case the music business didn't pan out. "I remember I was driving to college and I decided that at that moment, I was a guitarist. I was no longer a guitar student. My mother had taught me how to live off of rice and beans and I didn't need all those frivolous things like a house and a car that's all one color. I decided I was going to do whatever it took to be a guitarist so I quit my piano tuning apprenticeship and put everything into the guitar."

At DePaul, Anderson studied with Leon Borkowski, a former student of renowned classical guitarist Christopher Parkening, himself a direct link back to Andrés Segovia. "I always just loved the sound of Parkening's guitar and his expression. I learned a lot of Parkening's really beautiful arrangements like *Sheep May Safely Graze,* she recalls. "In order to play those, it took some very big stretches. I had to learn how to allow my hands to relax in order to make those stretches. The way I stretch is a little bit different – I stretch with the very tip of my fingers – it's the only way to get that relaxation. You don't want to go to the point of pain. It's important to listen to what your body's saying."

Borkowski wasn't a "touchy-feely" teacher. At one of her first lessons, he told her "You have a terrible tone. Come back when you can get a better tone and don't come back before that!" Anderson says this tough love approach was exactly what she needed to hear at the time.
She spent a week woodshedding every possible permutation on playing one note until she found her personal sound. "That was the most productive week of practicing I had in my life," she says. "It was a great approach for me, him challenging me and letting me discover a lot of the techniques on my own."

In her senior year at DePaul, Anderson was majoring in classical guitar but moonlighting in jazz and bluegrass bands. Though she enjoyed the challenges of changing genres on a daily basis, it eventually became tiring. She decided she would concentrate only on music with which she made a personal connection, regardless of genre. "I started playing just the music that made me happy", she explains. "Even though everyone told me I couldn't make a living doing that." Anderson played local concerts, hotel lobby gigs, wherever people would be willing to hire an unknown instrumentalist who (at the time) didn't sing. Besides her association with Jethro & Chet, the turning point was Winfield.

"I didn't particularly like contests but I had a problem to solve: whenever I was listed in the paper as performing someplace, they would inevitably put "singer-songwriter." Because there was a picture of a girl with a guitar it was automatically assumed I was a singer-songwriter. I needed some sort of a title to say that I was a *guitarist* – not just someone who strums. So Winfield actually solved that problem. I was actually quite surprised and honored to have won."

Ironically, years after throwing down her guitarist-only gauntlet, Anderson has begun to sing two or three songs in each show. "A lot of the songs that I've written in the last four years just had words attached," she explains. " I went around looking for a singer for a while then finally realized I had to sing them myself."

She's now about halfway around the Lake and, unlike her cell phone, Muriel shows no signs of fatigue. Her career has several facets I want to explore but the guitarist in me wants to know how she composes such stunning, orchestral arrangements. Anderson replies, "I generally start with a tune or with a feel and then just see what it needs. The hardest thing is not what to add but how to make it as simple as possible and still get across everything that song wants to get across." But what about multi-layered, polyphonic stuff like her finger-busting bluegrass medley?

"When I first started working out that arrangement, I was just about at the point where I was ready to give up and say it couldn't be done," she replies. "Then I started to get it right for two or three notes in a row, then four notes in a row and then it all started to fall into place. It was a new technique I was developing with my right hand in order to do that so it took a little while to feel comfortable. It seems sometimes it's just not working and then somehow, by the end, it's like riding a bicycle."

Her skill as a composer and arranger has helped Anderson's career blossom over the years in unexpected ways. After her *Heartstrings* CD was played during a space shuttle mission, NASA invited her to their annual Fajita Fest in Houston. According to Anderson, "It was the only show where during intermission, I went out and got autographs from the audience! "

Muriel's unique blend of musical ability, personal charm, and a healthy dose of being in the right place at

the right time, led a small, serendipitous jam session to become an ongoing event of international renown: *Muriel Anderson's All-Star Guitar Night.* As Muriel recalls, it all started at the Chet Atkins Appreciation Society, the annual Nashville convention that began in 1983 to honor the musical legacy and multi-faceted career of that unique artist. During the 1993 convention, Muriel invited Chet Atkins, Thom Bresh, Phil Keaggy and others who'd played the event to hang out around the pool and jam. "Some of the best music of the entire week happened right there," she recalls. "So the next year, one of the players asked if I was going to do my pool party again and I said, "Why don't we just do it on stage?" We went to the Bluebird Café in Nashville and found to our surprise we had just as much fun on stage."

All-Star Guitar Night has continued to grow into a multi-venue, multi-city event funded by corporate and individual donors whose proceeds after expenses go toward putting instruments in the hands of disadvantaged children through the Music For Life Alliance (www.musicforlifealliance.com), the organization Muriel founded to help make music learning accessible to young people who might not otherwise be able to experience the educational, psychological, and social benefits of making music. The relationships Anderson developed through her work with ASGN and MFLA have brought forth many friendships with musicians like Larry Carlton, Duane Eddy, Stanley Jordan and French guitarist, Jean-Félix Lalanne.

Muriel confirms a Lalanne story shrouded in guitar legend and immortalized by cartoonist Justin Greene in his defunct *Musical Legends* strip for Tower Records' *Pulse!* Magazine. "I met Jean-Felix Lelanne at the Chet Atkins convention. He'd broken his fingernail so I cut off my thumbnail, glued it on to his fingernail, and he played the concert with it. We've recorded two CDs together since. We feel so much the same; we phrase the same way so it's like playing with my identical twin. I also really enjoy playing with Stanley," she says. "He's a brilliant and wonderful person with a totally different way of approaching music. Tommy Emanuel of course is at the top of the list. Everyone agrees universally that he's at the top of his game. Nobody has music running through his or her veins quite as deeply as Tommy. "

Ever attuned to her environment, Anderson stops our guitar-centric conversation in its tracks to appreciate the beauty of a herd of deer gliding past. She comes here often to appreciate the natural beauty of the state park and find inspiration in nature for her life and music. My inner guitar geek tells me this is a good time to change gears and talk about her guitars. I ask her about her first instrument.

"My first guitar was a half-sized classical guitar that I've since loaned to any number of nieces and nephews to learn on. My first good guitar was a steel string Guild. At the Newport Guitar Festival in Miami, a couple years ago, I walked to the end of the hallway to a display of historic instruments owned by the founder of the festival and there was my old ladies parlor guitar that I bought from my first guitar teacher. It had been sold and sold. I picked up, played it once and put it back in the display."

At the same show, Anderson experienced that "Aha" moment of guitar karma every musician hopes for where you find a special instrument that seems to speak directly to your musical soul. As Anderson tells it, "I was on my way to talk about getting a Flamenco guitar from Paris Banchetti [www.parisbanchetti.com] when I walked past this David Taylor [www.dtguitars.com] steel string parlor guitar and thought, "That's the most beautiful inlay I've ever seen on a guitar." "I picked it up and a sweet kindness just came out of this guitar. My breath was taken away. I thought, "That's the sound I've been searching for my whole life! That's my voice; right there. I told him to put a "sold" sign on it. I didn't even bargain," she says with a laugh.

In a goose bump-inducing coda to the story, Anderson learned that Taylor had attended one of her guitar workshops, gone right home to his workbench and drawn up the designs for this very guitar. He'd chosen the inlay image of a wild rose he'd noticed growing in his backyard because he thought it described Anderson's personality.

Muriel has been one of the most visible players in reviving the harp guitar, a turn-of-the-19th-century instrument that adds additional bass strings to the guitar's voice. Anderson's interest in harp guitars began back at DePaul when she was playing the Bach's cello suites. "They were just crying out for low, ringing bass notes," she says. "I had seen pictures of harp guitars and thought, "*That's* what it needs. Shortly thereafter, I went to a Michael Hedges concert because I'd heard that he played a harp guitar. I sat next to an older couple and it turned out they were writing a book on the Larsons guitars. They asked me if I would record the music for the book and I had the chance to play my first harp guitar. [*The Larsons' Creations - Centennial Edition: Guitars and Mandolins* by Robert Carl Hartman, published by Centerstream].

"Del Langejans built me my first harp guitar; a beautiful steel-string with rosewood back and sides and a cedar top. I also have a new 21-string nylon harp guitar made by Mike Doolin. I tune the bass strings in a scale going down from the 6th string. I'll vary that depending on what's needed in a specific song. Half step tuners are handy for that. GHS makes me a string set specific to my instruments."

Asked about her preferences, she replies, "There are many variables in the sound of a guitar, so there are exceptions to my general preferences of woods. For classical, Brazilian rosewood back and sides with cedar top has typically been my favorite sound. Now that I'm doing more flamenco inspired music, I'm enjoying spruce top and cypress or other lighter wood for the back and sides. For steel string guitars I prefer spruce tops. I can't play steel string guitars for very long. I have to play them for short periods of time and then sand my nails inbetween." On the road as well as on many of her recordings, Anderson turns to her Morris signature model steel string [built by Moridaira guitars, Japan]. "I have to confess to quite a bit of Guitar Acquisition Syndrome these days," she adds. "I just ordered a flamenco guitar in spruce and cypress from Paris Banchetti and two new guitars from my new favorite builder, David Taylor: a small steel-string harp guitar I can bring on the road and another ladies parlor guitar just like the one I have. I'd also love to have Linda Manzer build me a guitar some time." To amplify her guitars, Anderson uses D-Tar wavelength pickups [www.d-tar.com], with stereo pickups for the harp guitars. She runs these through a D-Tar equinox to adjust the mid frequencies via a three-band equalizer. "I

nearly always dip the EQ at 800Hz and also in the high mids", she says. "To add presence to a room, I add a very narrow band of 20K." Anderson records with a Dirk Brauner stereo microphone, calling it the best sound she's heard.

Having a predictable method of getting her preferred guitar tones is mandatory for a player who puts in as much road time as Anderson. Unlike some musicians, she draws energy from travel. "I take the time to enjoy my surroundings," she tells me. "Whenever possible, if there's some beautiful place to visit, I'll take the time to do so – as I'm doing right now – walking around the beautiful lake with deer running on either side. I also really enjoy meeting people. I stay with families much more than I stay in hotels. I'm a bit of a gourmet. I like to experience the cuisine of the area and appreciate really good food in general. There's even a whole section on my website, "Recipes from the Road." I really enjoy getting to know the people and I try to learn a little bit of the language each place I go. I've really been enjoying learning German lately. Tomorrow I'm trading a guitar lesson for a German lesson. "

Recently, Muriel has been putting those German lessons to good use and having the time of her life playing flamenco music with the German guitar duo Tierra Negra [Raughi Ebert & Leo Henrichs]. "I met them at a guitar festival at a castle in Germany," she explains. "Before long we started jamming and played late into the night. We started realizing that there was something really special happening. They're brilliant in knowing how to create the greatest feel without adding too much. It's been a wonderful experience to work with musicians who really understand when to be minimal and when to break out. Since we started playing music together, I've had a lot more music come out in my dreams; it just opened up the floodgates to new tunes."

Anderson reunited with the duo to record *New World Flamenco*, a collaborative CD of original music. "Each of us wrote a third of the material. There's their Nuevo Flamenco sound and I'm playing my harp guitar on some pieces. It turned out to be a beautiful combination. The slow, beautiful pieces really stand out in the context of the joyous Spanish sounding pieces. When I first heard Tommy Emmanuel's music a light bulb went off: "Ah! That's the joy of music." The same thing happened when I met Tierra Negra."

In Anderson's view, it's this spirit of continuous inspiration and reawakening that helps her keep that joy of making music alive. At this point in our conversation, Muriel's trip around the lake has come full circle, an apt metaphor for a musician whose entire career has been calligraphed with curved brushstrokes; inclusive of the past but looking forward to the next bend in the road. Anderson plans to continue to share this generosity of spirit in her concerts and teaching. "I've chosen the long road in a lot of ways," she says with a chuckle. "I feel compelled to share my knowledge and what I've been able to pick up to make it a shorter road for other people. I believe that sharing knowledge is an integral part of giving back as a musician."

§

Three Godfathers: Jethro, Chet & Les

Having just *one* famous musician offer you sage advice, de facto music lessons and a turbo boost to your career is a lofty goal for anyone. In Anderson's case, *three* legendary players contributed to raising her career profile.

As a college student at De Paul University, Anderson decided to take lessons with mandolin legend Jethro Burns who taught in nearby Evanston, Illinois. "I went to mandolin lessons with Jethro more for humor lessons than anything else," she recalls. "He was *so* funny." Anderson's mother had often played *Nola*, a finger-busting novelty ragtime piano piece composed in 1915 by Felix Arndt. After hearing Anderson's virtuoso guitar arrangement of the tune, Burns introduced her to his brother-in-law, Chet Atkins. Chet started sending cassette tapes of tunes for her to learn for her hotel gigs and Anderson responded in kind with tapes of her latest compositions. She began to visit Nashville, stopping by Chet's office for an impromptu lesson whenever possible. Anderson recorded Chet's composition *To Be or Not to Be* before *he* did.

"Chet was very unassuming", she remembers. "It was like talking to your uncle. He always had a foot firmly planted on the ground on which he grew up. He had friends ranging from the man who sold T-shirts out of the back of his truck to former presidents and treated them all the same. He always treated other musicians with a lot of respect and was always complimenting other musicians. He was always looking to learn new things, especially from younger players."

Les Paul came into Muriel's life in an equally unexpected manner. "I was playing a live late night radio show in Chicago on WGN – the Steve & Johnnie show. It was about one o'clock in the morning and they said, "There's a caller on line one. It's Les Paul." I said, "Okay, who is it *really* – you're pulling my leg." He came on the radio and said, "I really like your playing and if you're ever in New York on a Monday night come and sit in and play with me." So I did, a half a dozen times, at least. Les was always there with a joke. Always keeping you laughing."

Contrary to expectations, Anderson found playing with these legendary guitarists to be a pressure-less situation. "You knew that they were there to support you and I could feel that support as I played so it wasn't intimidating. It was joyful."

§

GEORGE BARNES

A *groundbreaking guitarist's daughter opens a window into her father's life as a musician, husband and father.*

Les Paul, Chet Atkins and Charlie Christian's contributions to the history of the electric guitar are well known and often acknowledged. George Barnes, however, is rarely mentioned in the same sentence with these guitar legends although he influenced all three and was likely the first to record commercially on standard electric guitar (Hawaiian steel guitarists were the first electric musicians on record). In recent years, Barnes' contributions to American music and awe-inspiring versatility have been in the spotlight more often. How many guitarists could rightly claim to have played amazing solos on classic blues, jazz, country and rock & roll recordings?

Born in 1921 and raised in Chicago, Barnes was a guitar prodigy who turned pro at age 12. Greatly influenced by blues guitarist Lonnie Johnson, he ultimately found his muse in the playing of horn and reed players like cornetist Bix Beiderbecke and clarinetist Jimmie Noone. Barnes' older brother Reggie built him one the earliest guitar amplifiers and Barnes unique electric guitar voice was born: definitive pick attack, liquid, horn-like phrasing, clear, bell-like tone and a signature vibrato that made his notes shimmer like heat waves on a blacktop highway. By 1938, Barnes was recording commercially with blues icons like Big Bill Broonzy, and at 17, was hired as the youngest staff arranger at NBC in Chicago. He became a featured artist on national radio as both a soloist and the lead voice of his pioneering octet that featured moonlighting wind players from the Chicago symphony.

After moving to New York, his Jazz career flourished at night while Barnes became one of the most sought-after studio musicians in Manhattan, playing on countless hits for country, rock & roll and pop artists like Sam Cooke, Jackie Wilson, Paul Anka, Bobby Darin, Frank Sinatra, and even Bob Dylan.

A perfectionist to the core, Barnes' greatest satisfaction came from playing and recording his own music. In the 1960s, his duos with guitarists Carl Kress and Bucky Pizzarelli and cornetist Ruby Braff produced a number of classic swing jazz LPs. In 1975, Barnes' was enjoying a fertile new creative period in California as a player and teacher when he died suddenly of a heart attack at the age of 56. After a storied 44-year career in music, it seemed that Barnes' legacy was over. Enter Alexandra Barnes Leh, his daughter. A former vocalist and composer,

Leh spent ten years as a development executive at CBS Television and is now an independent producer and writer. With the advent of the internet, she and her mother, Evelyn Barnes, realized the tremendous worldwide interest in George Barnes' music.

Over several years, Leh and her mother organized and curated a collection of previously unavailable material from the family's private collection and also renewed available copyrights on his commercial teaching materials and recordings. These are the recorded music, compositions, arrangements, teaching methods, photographs, documents, and video and film footage that Barnes fans could only hope to find on auction sites. Now, all this is available from Barnes' heirs and generously supplemented with personal anecdotes - a rare opportunity to study the life and work of a highly influential musician.

§

What motivated you and your late mother to release the Legacy Collection now, almost 30 years after your father's passing?

It was in '97 and '98 that I first got online and discovered that people were very interested in him. It's heartening to me because it tells me is that there are people of all ages who appreciate true genius and are hungry for it and I want to feed a little of that hunger if I can. I see the Legacy Collection as an antidote to the cheapening and the devaluation of artistry. The process of true creation can only be appreciated and learned from when you're observing it in masters. It's incredibly important to hear a true artist's process to gain a deeper understanding of a completely committed creator. People in younger generations don't understand what it is to be a truly committed artist because the level of appreciation for creativity today is more about money than it ever was and not about the actual art. Entertainers in Dad's time were valued more than they are now or valued in a different way. We're in the middle of a period of reality ad nauseam. Seeing cute cuddly cats and people trying to sing is very entertaining but it's not true art; not what I understand creation to be.

Your Dad turned pro at a very young age.

Yes, Dad got his union card at 12 by special dispensation of the local Chicago union. He started on piano when he was 4. My grandfather was a piano maker and there was a piano in the house that Grandfather made. Dad studied with a piano teacher and he was brilliant on piano - and in fact, I have a recording that is part of the Legacy Collection that will come out in the second release. People love to know about the origins of what they love. How did it start?

Your dad was incredibly busy with his playing career for many years. What motivated him to begin teaching in the 1960s?

Dad thought it was the perfect time because everybody was picking up a guitar. They just wanted to play along with Simon and Garfunkel and the Beatles and everybody was exploring the instrument on an amateur level. Dad wanted all of us to learn - not just how to play guitar - but be musicians. He never ever included tablature because he thought it was a cheat. When he was working with young guitarists he taught them formal music. He believed they needed to know what note they were playing not just where to put their finger on the fretboard. Many guitarists don't know how to read [music] and that was anathema to Dad. The first book he wrote was in 1942 and it was released in '43 by Willam J. Smith – a company that no longer exists. We'll be releasing that as well.

George Barnes' LP *Country Jazz* was a seminal record for a lot of players. Danny Gatton is reported to have memorized the entire record.

We have re-released *Country Jazz*. I remember when Dad was working on it. It was originally on the Colortone label, which no longer exists. They were all his arrangements [of traditional tunes] and there were a couple of originals. He usually had one or two originals on any of his recordings.

I was very little, but I remember him working on it. It was a record he did because he thought it would be fun; it wasn't something he did to further his career. It was almost an homage to the work he did with Homer and Jethro in the '40s. People still quote Dad from those sessions. He told the other musicians: "If *you* don't make any mistakes there won't be any." He said that a lot and he was right.

What was it like growing up in Manhattan with a guitar genius for a father?

Mom and Dad moved to New York in 1951 because Milt Gabler, who owned Decca records, was a fan of his and wanted to sign him. At the same time, Bing Crosby wanted him to come out to Los Angeles. After they got married in '47, Mom and Dad drove out to LA to meet with Bing's leader at the time but Dad didn't like LA. He was a city boy from Chicago and LA didn't feel right.

I love having grown up in New York. We lived a block away from Central Park on 58th and 7th and catty corner from Carnegie Hall. New York was the most wonderful playground any child could have. I went to school with

the kids of painters and writers and musicians. In that way, it was rarified but we didn't know it then. After school, if I didn't go home, I'd go to Jim and Andy's – the bar where all of the musicians hung out. It was a great place. Jimmy was a family man. Mom and Dad put the phone number for Jim and Andy's on my emergency contact form at school. There were no cell phones then so if they couldn't be reached, it was "Call Jim. He'll know what to do."

Did your Dad have an easy professional transition from Chicago to New York?

Well, he couldn't do studio work in New York for a few months. His Chicago Union Card wasn't transferable. He ended up playing with Raymond Scott's orchestra on the Hit Parade. That's where he met the brilliant double bassist Jack Lessberg and the drummer, Cliff Lemon. They became fast buddies and eventually, all played on lots of studio dates together on the most famous rock & roll records. They later became the key members of the Jazz Renaissance Quintet.

Did George live and breathe music when he was at home?

Music was in our lives all the time and he loved playing guitar but Dad didn't really study music because he'd already done that when he was a kid. He didn't practice unless he was rehearsing a specific, complex piece. He said, "I don't need to practice, I'm always playing." But because his childhood had been so music-centric, he had a lot of other interests like astronomy. As a kid he'd read *Buck Rogers in the 21st Century* and would dream about what that would be like. He was a huge fan of President Kennedy because Kennedy was going to "get us into space." Dad was also a huge baseball fan. We went to all the Mets games.

I understand that he was a bit of a perfectionist when it came to music.

Dad *was* a perfectionist and he expected the best from anyone with whom he worked. Back in Chicago, when he led the George Barnes Octet, the players were for the most part from the Chicago Symphony. Dad had to teach them how to swing and it used to drive him a little bit crazy, apparently. If Mom was there at rehearsal, they'd send her out of the room so she wouldn't have to hear Dad dressing down the musicians (laughs). He couldn't tolerate musical laziness; if you didn't know it, that's one thing but if you knew it and you didn't play it, that was unconscionable to him.

Which guitarists did he admire?

All the guys who you'd expect a guitar player to love, but I'd venture that Carl Kress was his favorite. He loved Tal Farlow's playing and Bucky Pizarelli's. When Bucky picked up the 7-string he thought that was magical. He also heard it as a way to replicate Carl's tuning [Note: Carl Kress used a unique tuning derived from the plectrum banjo: Low to high Bb, F, C, G, B, D]. When he recorded *Guitar Galaxy* and *Guitars Galore* in the early 1960s for Mercury's *Perfect Present Sound,* several of his favorite guitarists were on those recordings with him: Bucky, Billy Bauer, Don Arnone, Everett Barksdale, Carl Kress, and Barry Galbraith – the cream of the New York studios at that time. But the truth is, he didn't really listen all that much to other guitarists because he was either playing with them daily or wanting to take a break from the guitar by listening to classical music or doing things like reading the funnies on a Sunday afternoon. He'd put on Duke Ellington, Louis Armstrong, Art Tatum, or anything his colleagues had just done. Dad listened to classical music as much if not more than he listened to jazz.

Studio players often have many guitars so they're prepared to handle many different genres. Did your Dad own many instruments?

Dad didn't like to own a lot of guitars. He said, "I can only play one at a time." He often gave them away. He gave Bucky a D'Angelico; he gave the Gibson he'd played on the Octet records to his brother Harry, who was also a great guitar player. He gave all of the F Guitars* away. I recall that one went to [jazz guitarist] Sal Salvador.

That's why he designed the Acousti-Lectric, 'cause he didn't want to own a lot of guitars. Dad loved Chet Atkins playing and George was one of Chet's idols. After Dad died Chet came to LA, called me and invited me to his concert. I brought Dad's Acousti-lectric guitar. He played it a little bit backstage and said "Do you mind if I have it on stage with my other guitars?" At one point he got up, walked over to the guitar and started playing it and talking about Dad. He did 20 minutes on Dad including a little bit of "Something Tender," a composition of Dad's Chet had recorded on his album *From Nashville With Love.* As great as Chet was, it didn't sound anything like Dad.

George had a unique sound and approach to single note playing that was much more truly horn-like than many other jazz guitarists, such as Herb Ellis and Barney Kessel, who professed to be influenced by horn players.

That's right. I was recently talking with Mom about Johnny Mercer. Dad and Bucky were playing at Dante's in Los Angeles the night before the big earthquake in '71. Johnny Mercer [legendary songwriter] walked in and said, "Who's playing that clarinet?" Of course, it wasn't a clarinet, it was Dad.

People who know Barnes as a consummate swing jazz musician may be surprised that he was a part of so many famous pop and rock sessions.

Yes, many of the young players I talk with cite the Octet and *Country Jazz* as the most influential things he did but he did so much else! It's such a long list. Next time I'm in New York, I'm going to go back to the AFM and get that list of everything Dad played on. In the '50s and '60s he was one of the busiest guitarists in New York. He was playing on everything from pop sessions to Pepsi and Alka Seltzer jingles.

What are the most well known records that feature Barnes?

Almost anything that [legendary producer/writers] Hugo & Luigi or Leiber and Stoller produced; if they could get George, they'd call him first. Paul Anka, Neil Sedaka – all that early stuff; Sam Cook's New York recordings; the Coasters. Dad's on Bobby Vinton's *Blue Velvet* and *Dream Lover* with Bobby Darin. I hear him all the time. I was at the Blue Velvet session. I was 8 years old. When I was 9, Mom and Dad were guests on the Arthur Godfrey show and he brought Mom and me on stage. I did an orange juice commercial with Godfrey and Dad had just taught me how to play the tenor ukulele. I'd learned *It Ain't Gonna Rain No More, No More*"and Godfrey said, "Can you play it for me?" and handed me his baritone uke. So I started playing the right notes but I was singing it in the key I'd learned it in. Dad and Godfrey and Carl Kress roared with laughter. He and Carl were the closest possible friends and they were such a complete musical entity together. After Carl died, there was a whole chunk of time that was really awful for Dad. It was like losing a brother.

George and Carl Kress had almost a telepathic relationship as a guitar duo. After Kress died, he partnered with Bucky Pizarelli, but the unique magic of the previous partnership was hard to recapture.

It was the '60s, and Dad was not a fan of the popular music of the time except for the Beatles. It was *Here There and Everywhere* that turned him around. I loved it when they got together because they'd known each other for a long time. Even though Dad and Bucky were wonderful together, and made great music together, Dad was never able to replicate the personal and professional relationship he had with Carl ever again. I think that hurt him quite a bit. My Mom and I believe it broke his heart. I don't think I'm speaking out of turn when I say that Bucky was a proponent of playing the more popular stuff. That was just a smart business move. That's how you got more airplay - younger people listening to you. I completely understand it but Dad *hated* it. It was the reason that they broke up. Albert Grossman outlined their breakup in an article for New York Magazine in about 1972. They broke up on stage at the St. Regis Room.

Dad was a really opinionated guy. He had very, very specific ideas of what was good and what wasn't. He would always do his best to make what wasn't good better. If he were here now I'd bet he'd say, "Gee, I could have pulled back on that." The fact is they both loved each other's playing and had a long history together.

In addition to the *Legacy Collection*, you've remastered and released on CD your Dad's incredible arrangement of the Bach Fugue in G Minor with his group *The Jazz Renaissance Quintet*. It's such a joyful performance and so cool that you included all the retakes, studio outtakes and chatter.

Dad enjoyed listening to Brahms, Beethoven, Mozart, Respighi, Ravel, Mussorgsky, Tchaikovsky, Wagner and Bach. The original session took place in February 1962 at A&R Recording. With the Bach Fugue, those were five masters of their art: George, Hank, Bucky, Cliff, Jack. [guitarist Bucky Pizzarelli, clarinetist Hank D'Amico, bassist Jack Lesberg and drummer Cliff Leeman]. Nobody was better than they were at that point. To hear them having fun and Dad saying, "Okay, okay let's keep it moving", you can hear all the nuances; the love and respect and the shorthand. I love the shorthand of creation. I grew up with that. And running the board and co-producing with Dad was [late legendary recording engineer] Phil Ramone. How are you going to get better than that?

Part of the real impact of the *Legacy Collection* is the way it introduces us to George Barnes as a complete human being, not just as a musician and guitar icon.

Dad loved being a family man because it kept him grounded. He was married twice before he married my Mom. He was first married at 17. His first wife was a singer. They met at 16 but her father wouldn't let them marry until he had a job so that's when he became staff arranger for the NBC Orchestra in Chicago. He was married again at 21 to another "girl singer." Dad's second wife introduced my mother to Dad.

Dad had a first heart attack that hospitalized him in '74. I was working in pop A&R at RCA Records – in fact it was my first day – when I got the call to come to the hospital. He didn't want to acknowledge that there was anything wrong with his body when there was so much right with his mind. There was a real disconnect there and I think that's true for a lot of creative people. Dad was only 56 years old when he died. He had fulfilled a great many of his promises. Even though he'd had a 44-year career, 56 was too young, especially given everything that he was going to do.

Dad loved to be happy and make others happy and loved it when his wife and his little girl were happy. He was a fan of the Marx Brothers and Laurel and Hardy. He was one of the most tender hearts I've ever known. I want people to love his music but I want them to know why they love his music.

Except for the Army, Dad never made a living doing anything but music. Whenever he received a compliment like "Mr. Barnes, I love the way you play" or "I'm such a fan" he'd always say, "Then you are obviously a person of impeccable taste."

The George Barnes Legacy Collection: www.georgebarneslegacy.com
Bach Fugue in G Minor CD: http://theartofsoundgallery.com/site/gallery/bach-fugue-in-gm

§

GINO BORDIN

You know the story: the scene is Paris is the early 1930s. A uniquely talented guitarist emerges onto the music scene commanding the attention of both audiences and his fellow musicians. His abilities help make him a fixture in the city's cabarets and nightclubs and a star on recordings and radio. No, we're not talking about Django. The guitarist in question is Gino Bordin.

At the same time that Reinhardt and Grappelli were just starting what would become their unique musical legacy, an alternate scene was happening in 1930s Paris, fueled not by Louis Armstrong and the beat of American Swing, but by the languid sounds of the Hawaiian Islands. At the center of this movement was Gino Bordin, at the right place and time in a city crazy for exotic culture and music.

Born in Bolzano, Italy in 1899, Bordin began to play music at an early age, performing on guitar, banjo, and even the musical saw. He moved to France in 1926 where, though he struggled initially, he eventually triumphed to become a fixture in the clubs, beer halls, cinemas, and variety revues of Paris. On any given night, one might find Bordin, like Django, accompanying an accordionist on a six-string banjo or, dressed as an Argentine Gaucho, holding down the guitar chair in a Tango orchestra. The next night might find him decked out in a white suit and lei leading his own Hawaiian Orchestra. This kind of versatility earned Bordin a reputation as a consummate professional, capable of performing in a wide variety of styles.

Though Bordin played standard guitar and musical saw throughout his long career, it's his work on Hawaiian steel guitar that's best remembered today. His style was precise yet emotional, with a wide vibrato and staccato attack similar to that of Frank Ferera, a Hawaiian of Portuguese decent who was the most prolifically recorded of the earliest Hawaiian steelers. Though Ferera never visited Europe, his recordings were widely available there.

Interestingly enough, while Bordin and other Parisian guitarists learned to play Hawaiian style (with the guitar flat on their lap, tuned to an open chord and noted with a steel bar) they made few changes to their existing repertoire. Bordin's steel guitar slipped seamlessly into the accordion music of the mussette, the tango, sentimental ballads, Neapolitan songs, and light classical pieces.

He also composed his own tunes and recorded scores of 78 rpm records for the Odeon, Parlophone, Pathe, and Polydor labels under both his own name and the pseudonyms, Guy Ridon and Mac Gony. To further complicate things, Bordin often played and recorded with fellow Hawaiian guitarist Alex Manara whose style on the instrument was similar to Bordin's. The two were fixtures on Parisian radio in the '30s.

Whether playing with a full orchestra, playing duets with piano or another guitar or piano, Bordin was simply the best steel player in Paris. He was also an innovator. According to producer Cyril Lefebvre, Bordin was the first Parisian steel guitarist to add a 7th string. Bordin was a friend of the innovative luthier Mario Maccaferi and influenced his design of the Selmer Hawaiian model. Created in 1931, this model featured the large, D-shaped soundhole comparable to Selmer's orchestra models, soon to become iconic thanks to Django Reinhardt. The guitar had a raised nut, a wide, flat fingerboard and the Macaferri-designed internal soundbox. It was offered with either 6 or 7 strings and featured heavier bracing to offset the increased tension of lap-style tunings. According to Selmer expert Francois Charle, the 7-string model was actually a modified 6-string. In order to accommodate the extra string, the tailpiece was split down the middle and a piece of metal then welded in. The Hawaiian model was not a success and was quickly abandoned by 1932. In 1934, Bordin acquired a National 7-string electric lap-steel. He used it on his recording of *J'ai mis mon coeur dans ces roses,* probably the first recording of the electric guitar in France.

During World War II Bordin somehow managed to gig with his group throughout Europe, even playing widely in Germany and Poland. After the war he extended his travels to Switzerland, Greece, Egypt and Monte Carlo. Bordin's popularity crossed over into the LP era and his recordings appeared on labels such as Mondo and Vogue. His creativity even extended to inventing. He devised and briefly tried to market, a system of cards in plastic trays that showed voicings for over 580 guitar chords. In 1935, Bordin published a method book called *A New Practice Method for Hawaiian Guitar.*

He supplemented his income with teaching for most of his career, continuing to do so until his death from a series of heart attacks in 1977. Largely forgotten today, Gino Bordin nevertheless played a seminal role in popularizing the steel guitar in Europe. Some of his best work, along with rare photos, can be found on the compilation CD, *Paris, Plages D'Hawaii* produced by the late French collector and Bordin connoisseur, Cyril LeFebvre (Universal France 983-643-5).

The author is indebted to Cyril Lefebvre, Gerrit Venema, and Les Cook for their assistance with this article.

§

JERRY BYRD

Jerry Byrd was one of the most accomplished steel guitarists in the history of the instrument. He almost singlehandedly created and defined the steel guitar sound of the records coming out of Nashville in the late 1940s & early '50s. His trademark vibrato, impossibly-perfect intonation and variety of lush tunings became the blueprint for a generation of steel guitarists. His approach to Hawaiian music become a touchstone for musicians, film composers, and advertising alike during the '50s & '60s. When Byrd's remarkable playing first hit the airwaves, musicians were nonplussed. Many players wrote to him to ask how he was getting those sounds. Byrd made it a point of pride to always write back. Throughout his life he answered his fan mail and shared his knowledge and point of view. Here's how Byrd explained how he developed his unique diatonic tuning:

"I experimented with various tunings in the years following my discovery of C6th tuning in 1937, but all of them were unplayable. Having gone to a 7-string guitar in the mid '40s so I could add the much needed C note that was eliminated when I raised the 6th string to C#, I then had C and C# to work with.

I kept hearing a chord in my head that I know would give me a new dimension and after much twisting and turning of tuning keys and changes of string gauges, I found it - this was sometime in the early '50s. I ended up with the alphabet. The formula came out, from bottom to top, as: E-F-G-A-B-C (D)-E. I have the D in parenthesis because it completely made the whole thing unplayable and was only in the way – and besides, I'd need an 8-string neck. So, off it came and so I ended up with E to E without the D. And my lost chord was there on the 6th, 5th, 4th, 3rd and 1st strings. And I still had my E and C on top.

It took me awhile to realize that I really had something! I could do all I ever did in my C6th tuning and much more. It was great for popular songs, because I could play most everything in 3-part harmony with my ever-present slants and it was equally good for Hawaiian and country. I kept it under wraps for 2 or 3 years, which was easy because I was about as much in demand as yesterday's newspaper but I kept working with it.

One day, my phone rang and it was Ferlin Huskey. He said, "I'm doing a session soon and I want you to play steel. I said, "Are you sure you called the right number?" He said, "Damn right!! And I want you to play Jerry Byrd and don't let anybody try to change anything." I said, "Well okay, I'll be there!" At the session he came over to me and said, "Now I want you to play Jerry Byrd on this next song titled *Next to Jimmy.* I said, "Give me a few minutes to see if I can remember what Jerry Byrd did." I then worked up the first recording I ever did in that [diatonic] tuning and it is still talked about. I am continually reminded of it. Know what? I have not the slightest idea of what I played. I'd play and go home and forget about it. That's the way we did it. "

§

CINDY CASHDOLLAR

It's Saturday night at the Fitzgerald Theater in St. Paul, Minnesota and another live broadcast of Minnesota Public Radio's popular *A Prairie Home Companion*. As Garrison Keillor wraps up his trademark riff on the virtues of powder milk biscuits, Cindy Cashdollar kicks off a swinging version of the western swing classic, *Boot Hill Drag*.

Live radio is just the latest step in a musical odyssey of resophonic and lap steel guitar that's taken her around the world, garnered five Grammy awards, and made her one of the most visible and respected lap-style guitarists around. From eight swinging years with *Asleep At The Wheel*, to recordings and gigs with Bob Dylan, Leon Redbone, *Beausoleil, Manhattan Transfer*, Peter Rowan, Graham Parker, Kelly Willis, Rosie Flores, and Jorma Kaukonen, Cashdollar displays a chameleon-like ability to fit seamlessly into diverse musical settings.

She credits her upbringing in the New York Catskill mountain town of Woodstock - an important musical crossroads long before its rock festival fame - for her early exposure to a wide variety of American music. "There was a club called the *Joyous Lake* where I saw people like Bonnie Raitt, Sonny Terry and Brownie McGee, Muddy Waters, Willie Dixon and Pinetop Perkins. I was hearing Happy and Artie Traum, *The Band*, and John Hammond, Jr. If you were 14 or 15 years old you could walk into places and nobody carded you."

After starting with blues fingerpicking on standard guitar, Cindy made the switch to resophonic guitar and the next few years saw her gigging and touring with bluegrass legend John Herald, Levon Helm and Rick Danko of *The Band*, and blues raconteur Leon Redbone. "Mike Auldridge, Josh Graves and Tut Taylor were my biggest inspirations when I was learning the Dobro", says Cindy. "I got into playing steel from Mike's *Eight-String Swing* album because he was using a 6th tuning on an eight-string so I tried to adapt that to my six-string Dobro.

I had played single-neck lap steel in G tuning for a long time with Levon, Rick and Paul Butterfield. I was kind of dabbling with a double-8 string steel but hadn't really done much with it when *Asleep At The Wheel* came along in '92. The *Wheel* was the greatest education anybody could have asked for. It was western swing boot camp for someone who was familiar with the style but had never played it. It kind of threw me into high gear because I really had to do it and do it quickly, in order to keep up in such an incredible band."

Since leaving *Asleep At The Wheel* in 2001, she has plunged headlong into a busy national freelance career in a wide variety of roots music settings, as well as teaching workshops and recording four instructional videos for *Homespun Tapes*. "I love getting to play in new situations with different people such as Jorma Kaukonen. Working with him as much as I did last year, it was so amazing to be that close to his guitar playing all the time. He's got a beautiful style and I found myself being greatly influenced by his guitar playing. I like things that have a texture to it."

Vocalist and Gulf Coast blues piano dynamo, Marcia Ball sums up the opinion of many musicians: "It's so easy to admire Cindy. I've seen her play western swing, big band, country, blues and rockabilly, on steel, dobro, and slide guitar. She's flawless, with a ton of technique and great instincts."

Queried about her current projects, Cindy relates her excitement over the February 2004 release of *Slide Show* (available from www.texasmusicroundup.com), her first CD under her own name. The disc features a musical potluck of some of the best contemporary musicians in acoustic music: "The guest musicians are all people who were inspirations and people that I admired forever: Sonny Landreth, Jorma Kaukonen, Herb Remington, Steve James, Lucky Oceans, Redd Volkaert, Artie Traum, Jay Unger & Molly Mason, Johnny Nicholas, Marcia Ball and Mike Auldridge. According to Auldridge, "Working on her new CD was really a lot of fun for me, because I got to play some eight-string songs and watch her do her part on a six-string harmonizing my parts, scrambling for licks that are much easier on an eight-string, and just *burning* me in the process. She's a terrific player and person."

Asked why she remains attracted to the sound of a steel bar on strings, Cindy says, "I love the vocal expression and textures that come from slide guitar and the fact that you have a kind of control/not control thing that goes on. It's like riding a wave and drifting with the current." And yes, Cashdollar is her real name.

§

AMOS GARRETT

Amos Garrett was born in Detroit and raised in Toronto. He tried piano and trombone lessons before finding the guitar at age 14. Within a year, he was gigging. By the time he'd reached college age, Garrett was deep into early acoustic Delta blues players like Robert Johnson but had an ear open to rock, country and jazz. He worked hard to develop his own sound, playing in Toronto bar bands and backing up singers like the acoustic folk duo Ian and Sylvia Tyson. Garret's first big career break came as a member of their touring and recording band. Garrett was strongly influenced by classic jazz but filtered through a rock and roll lens. It was at this time, playing in country-rock and folk-rock bands, that he began developing his unique approach to string bending – phrasing melodies and chords in such a way that the notes seemed to melt together in the manner of a pedal steel guitarist. This technique demands a keen ear for intonation and fingers of steel.

Garrett coupled these capabilities to a wonderful feeling for melody and great taste, knowing when to lay out and when to play. He became a skilled guitar player able to contribute to many genres of music and one whose sound was becoming increasingly identifiable on record. It was Garrett's intro and guitar solo on Maria Muldaur's 1974 hit, *Midnight at the Oasis* that made Garrett a cult figure among other guitarists. Players were amazed at the way his solo melded jazz phrasing with melting, multi-note bends and sliding double stops that dovetailed perfectly with the song's languid harmonies.

Since then, Garrett has played with over 150 well-known artists like Stevie Wonder, Emmylou Harris, Bonnie Raitt and Anne Murray (with whom he recorded her first five albums). He began to sing at gigs and on recordings and has added his fine bass baritone voice to the jazz, blues, country and rock he performs for audiences today.

Garrett moved to Alberta, Canada in 1989 and keeps busy with his acoustic act, blues band and a jazz trio. Over more than four decades in the music business, Amos Garrett has solidified his reputation as one of the most singular and tasteful players ever to pick up an electric guitar.

You're justly famous for your string bending skills – pushing or pulling strings to alter the pitch of as many as three notes at a time. How did you first become interested in the technique?

Steel guitar really influenced me in a lot of my string bending thing. My first major gig in my career, when I started to tour nationally and internationally, was with Ian and Sylvia Tyson in what was probably the prototypical country rock band, *The Great Speckled Bird*. That was the first time I ever played with pedal guitar players. We had a great steel player named Buddy Cage. I thought if I could double or harmonize some of Buddy's figures it would make for a very interesting guitar/pedal guitar relationship. That's when I started working on bending more than one string.

Your guitar solo on Maria Muldauer's Midnight At the Oasis comes up on many people's list of all-time greatest solos on pop records. How were you hired to play on the session?

I met Maria before she had a solo career, but after her time with the Jim Kweskin jug band. I met her in Toronto. After Kweskin, she and her ex-husband Geoff formed a band in Woodstock, NY that included me. They moved there because Albert Grossman had moved there and built a recording studio called Bearsville. We were sort of supported by Warner Brothers and we did two albums then Geoff and Maria got divorced and that was the end of that band.

Maria moved to the West Coast and I spent the better part of the next three years working with Paul Butterfield in Butterfield's last touring band, which was called *Butterfield's Better Days*. This was post-Bloomfield, Bishop, and Ralph Walsh – the guitar players that preceded me.

Anyhow, Maria and Geoff each got solo artist deals with Warner Brothers after they split up. They were very confident in Geoff but they had their doubts about Maria and they asked her to make a demo. She did a four-song demo at Bearsville and I played on the demo. One of the four songs on the demo was a new song by David Nichtern. He wrote *Midnight at the Oasis* in a water bed in a loft in the middle of a very hot day in New York City. He'd written the song very quickly and when he finished it, he instantly thought about Maria and called her on the spot. He said, "I've just written this song and it's hard to describe: lyrically, it leans toward the kind of Arabic, North African love songs of the 1930s and '40s but it's really an R&B tune." It's got a light, kind of half-time groove. I'll have to play it for you."

Fortunately for me, I got to play on the demo and she called me two and a half years later when she was making her first solo album for Warners. I was in LA playing at Douglas' Troubadour with Paul Butterfield. I went over to the studio (appropriately) around midnight and did the session for that one song. I played on the bed track and then there was a bunch of overdubbing to do. I was flying out to San Francisco with Butterfield the next morning. The solo was the first overdub.

It's a very unusual song in terms of chord structure and melody, especially the bridge. The solo was basically improvised other than one little run of triads that I'd previously worked out to play on another sort of North African song, *Lady of the Evening,* an old pop standard from the 1920s. Like *Sheik of Araby* and *When Rebecca Came Back from Mecca* - that whole lyrical style became popular in the 1920s apparently when air travel became a reality and a number of songwriters jumped on that theme.

What gear did you use on the song?

I probably used the house's twin amp because my amps were being lugged off to San Francisco that night by our roadies. The guitar I played was actually David Nichtern's electric. Nichtern and I played very similar guitars at that time. He played a Gibson ES-330, which is the predecessor to the ES-335/ES-350 line. The main difference being the pickups were different and it was completely hollow. I usually played an Epiphone Sheraton, also made by Gibson.

Nichtern and I also had the same luthier in NYC, Eddie Deal. Whenever Eddie set up a guitar he set it up the way he thought was perfect. You couldn't ask him to do anything custom or to your own taste but he was always right. He'd say, "I'll set it up so it's perfect and you let me know if you want any changes." So Nichtern's and my guitar were set up identically. The night that we did the session, I noticed my guitar was slightly out of tune at the 12th fret. It had just gotten a little out of whack on the road and I didn't want to take the time to adjust the bridge and the saddle. Nichtern was playing acoustic rhythm guitar on the session so I said, "David, my Sheraton's out of whack, can I use your 330?" He said, "Sure, it's in the trunk of my car." And that's the guitar I used.

How often are you asked about that record and that solo?

That recording was kind of like *The Little Engine that Could* in the children's story. Warner Brothers didn't initially perceive it as a single. It was the last song recorded for the album and they almost didn't record it because they had enough material already but Maria just loved the song and wanted it to go on the record. Nichtern didn't like my solo initially. He stuck around for my overdub and I think he thought it was too weird. He wanted something more mainstream.

Well, the label released two other singles off that album first and they both died. They almost deleted the entire album at one of their monthly meetings but Lenny, one of the co-producers, stood up and defended the album in front of the Warner executives. They said, "C'mon, we released two singles and they both died. The album's not selling." He said, "I just want to release one more single, *Midnight at the Oasis*. One of the presidents of Warner's said, "That's the best song on the record, it's my favourite song on the record but it's not a hit." Lenny said to him, "Did you hear what you just said? I've heard everybody in the Warner Brother's building say the same thing for six months."

They pressed up a couple of thousand and sent them out to the radio stations and two weeks later it was like "number ten with a bullet" and a couple weeks after that, it was number two on the worldwide charts and it stayed on the charts for something like seven months. Like *The Little Engine That Could,* it faced all these obstacles but finally went over the top of the mountain.

Is Midnight At The Oasis part of your shows today?

I did a tour of Japan this past Spring; 24 concerts in 24 days over there. The last few days of the tour, I did something I'd never done before. I've never sung *Midnight at the Oasis* in my act and I've never played it instrumentally but I've often thought there should be a way I could do that. It really is a woman's song and it sounds best being sung by a soprano. Near the end of this Japanese tour, one of the local promoters emailed me to say it was his life's dream to hear me play the solo from *Midnight at the Oasis* at his hall. He said, "I know you don't do it in your shows and I know it has to be played in the key of E because the solo's dependent on some open strings. I know you don't sing it in that key, but I have a female vocalist who's Polynesian and she does the song in her show and she does it in the key of E." Well, we did it as the encore at the end of the night and the place just went ballistic! It was quite amazing.

Today I look at it as kind of like a calling card. People still ask me about it, especially musicians I've just met for the first time. They've always got a few questions about that solo and how I did it. It's opened a lot of doors and it opened a lot of people's ears to my style in general and got them listening to other recordings I'd done. It's been a really good thing for me.

§

BEN HARPER

The essence of who Ben Harper is evident in every note he sings or plays. Whether lending his voice to a soul-stirring cover of a Bob Marley song, rocking an arena with a high-energy band performance or creating a cinematic vision on solo lap steel, Benjamin Chase Harper is a musical switch hitter. Over more than thirty years, he has repeatedly hit artistic home runs in several categories: as a songwriter, multi-instrumentalist, soulful vocalist and as a lap-style guitar player and valued collaborator in guitar design.

A three-time Grammy Award winner and seven-time nominee, Harper's eclectic mix of folk, blues, soul, reggae, and rock music has been a hit with critics as well as the listening public. While his nearly twenty recordings show remarkable stylistic range, he is equally renowned for his live performances with his band The Innocent Criminals" as well as his social activism outside of music. Well-known and respected in the United States, Harper is also a critical and audience favorite around the world. His 2008 collaboration "Boa Sorte/Good Luck" with Brazilian singer Vanessa da Mata peaked at #1 in Brazil and Portugal and his recordings receive frequent airplay in Europe and Australia.

Harper began playing the guitar as a child thanks to his maternal grandparents' ownership of the Folk Music Center and Museum, a seminal music store and gathering place for California musicians whose legacy he preserves as its current owner. He made the Weissenborn acoustic steel guitar a cornerstone of his style and has used his experiences in repairing and selling instruments at his family's store to collaborate with luthiers David Dart, Bill Asher and John Montelone. Harper's latest recording, "Winter is for Lovers" offers a spellbinding fifteen-movement solo steel performance, each section named for a specific place, from Istanbul to Islip—the Long Island town where John Monteleone designed and built Harper a unique archtop lap guitar.

Harper and I recently discussed a number of cherry picked highlights from his long career, the enduring appeal of lap steel, and how his new Montelone guitar inspired and challenged him as a musician.

What is it about lap style guitar that is so compelling to so many people?

There are at least a few reasons that jump to mind as to why lap steel guitar is so compelling. There's a very specific sound and feel which comes only from the instrument being horizontal. It has sonic elements of both piano and cello that are unique to lap style guitar. A lot of what I am playing on "Winter Is For Lovers" would typically be cello and piano lines. The boundaries of standard guitar have been consistently pushed for a while now, where I think there's still a lot of room for new and exciting sounds and styles from lap steel. Also, lap guitar is obviously a much different physical approach to guitar and one which I've always felt more comfortable with. To this day, lap steel still seem to be an outlier, but it has certainly made huge strides as far as recognition and awareness. People used to come up to me and say, "You're that guy who plays '*that thing*' on his lap", but I haven't heard that for a long time. Now they approach me and say, "Hey you're that guy who plays *guitar* on your lap". So at least now people seem to know that it's a guitar!

My impression is that, despite all your success, you seem to have retained that feeling of wonder and possibility that we all had as kids going into guitar stores – and you actually grew up in one – but you still seem to have a passion for instruments. Is this impression accurate?

Spot on accurate. The mystery seems to only grows deeper, my curiosity and awe surrounding instruments and tone feel as new and full of possibility as they did 30 years ago.

You and Bill Asher have really dialed in the original design you collaborated on and extended it from the original vision of a Weissenborn-influenced electrics to your Les Paul-influenced signature model. Briefly, what has that partnership been like and in your view, what is the "superpower" of these Asher guitars?

Billy and I came up with that design 25 years ago in his living room. By late 1995 in my attempt to integrate the Weissenborn into my own style of rock music, I had pushed the instrument to where the volume to feedback ratio was no longer controllable. There wasn't an acceptable wood 25" lap steel to be found, and the Asher was born.

The Asher Lap Steel offered new sonic potential at a different volume threshold at a time where I had run out of options. It has also found an exciting place to sonically exist with a clean tone as well. The song "All That Has Grown" showcases this. Of course nothing replaces the Weissenborn for a certain sound and feel.

The partnership has been great and it's still evolving. What makes the Asher lap steel stand out both sonically and aesthetically, is the care that Billy individually puts into each one. He deeply loves his craft and you can hear it and see it in every instrument he makes. It puts time into perspective in a crazy way for me when I think about the fact that the Weissenborn has been around 100 years, and the Asher has existed for 25 of those.

∞

Your recording "Winter is For lovers" features solo performances on an acoustic lap steel built by renowned archtop mluthier John Monteleone. This was his first lap steel. How did that collaboration happen, what did you hope to achieve, what unique features are on this guitar, and what was your reaction when you held the finished guitar for the first time?

I wandered in to Rudy's Guitars in SOHO New York, and one of the great things about Rudy's is that you can play some of the finest instruments ever made, as well as nerd out on them up close and personal. I found myself in the vintage arch top section, and began to play D'Angelico's and D'Aquisto's. Growing up in a guitar store myself, I have an appreciation for guitars of all styles, but there was always something deeply mysterious and sonically rewarding about arch-top guitars.

While I was playing, Rudy handed me a guitar, and without looking at it, I began to play. I was immediately struck by the tone. I couldn't sonically tell if it was an arch-top or a flat top until I took a close look at it. It was an arch-top that completely covered the acoustic sonic spectrum in a way I had never heard before. This is what began my quest to connect with John Monteleone.

I wanted exactly what I heard in Rudy's that day, but in a lap guitar: the bell type clarity and projection on the high end, which tend to be arch top characteristics, with the richness and warmth on the low end, more traditionally found in flat top guitars. Most important of all - "the spook" -the intangible tone quest that keeps guitar players perpetually hurling towards the sonic mystery, in hopes of finally arriving at the creative unknown.

It's honoring the tree the instrument came from. Tell the tree's story as well as your own. The roots, the soil, the wind, the perilous storms it withstood. To then be cut down in it's prime, stripped and shipped around the world. A century or two later, covered in lacquer and with 200 lbs of steel string pressure, the tree arrives in my arms, or in this case, in my lap.

The first time I held the finished guitar, I was in the same state of amazement I remain in today, which is that I not only have the guitar, but that it met and surpassed my every expectation.

How does it differ from the Weissenborns you're so well known for and how did it change or inspire what you wanted to play?

The Monteleone is a 25 1/2" scale with a carved top and back, compared to the Weissenborns 25" scale flat top and back. This immediately widened the playing field, opening up a new sonic landscape. Also the longer scale length brought about a much different physical responsiveness in the way the bar resonates and moves. It's a very rewarding guitar to play, and is hard for me to put down once I start playing it.

I have had the rare opportunity to put a nut riser on almost every type of guitar ever made. I realize with my deep connection to the Weissenborn, and the imaginative stretch that is the Monteleone, this might raise an eyebrow or two. I feel the album 'Winter Is For Lovers' answers any sonic questions or reservations in that regard. I wish you could've seen the look on [colletor/journalist] Ben Elder's face when he strummed it for the first time.

The Monteleone guitar's dynamic range – especially the lows and low mids - sounds huge, but not muddy on 'Winter is For Lovers'. There's sense of deliberate intention here. Each piece really seems to conjure a mood while staying free of any particular genre. How did you compose each piece - each titled for a different location?

First and foremost, John makes extraordinary sounding instruments. The sound I was reaching for was with absolute intention. And thank you for hearing this to the depth that you do. One of the most important sonic components to the Monteleone lap steel is the arched back. John, in his genius, carved the back so that the outermost point of the arched back has a subtle flatness to it, so the body of the instrument rests on a point, which allows the entire instrument to resonate freely and uninhibited.

'Winter Is For Lovers', is meant to be composed as one lap steel symphony. It is only segmented from one movement to the next because the record company felt it would sell better. I'll jump under the bus with them as I gave it the final ok. Allowing this to happen is something I regret. Once I foolishly agreed to let it be individually streamed, I decided to title them after the places that most deeply reflected my connection/memory to that specific piece. Many of the individual movements were written in the cities they are titled after.

Unusually for a lap steel player you don't use fingerpicks. How does that affect your approach to the instrument?

I've tried finger picks off and on over the years, but there's a specific dynamic range that disappears for me the second o put them in. I love listening to other players use them, but for myself, I can't find a place for them.

I understand you're a fan of Dumble amps. Is that something you picked up from David Lindley? What makes them special? And please give me a few thoughts about your relationship with Lindley. He influenced so many musicians.

When amps became an integral part of my electric sound around '95/'96, David was the most important point of reference when it came to electrified lap steel. Dumble - like Lindley - is a very rare and special human, and puts his entire being into what he does. This devotion is audible in his amps. I tend to sound almost exactly the same on every guitar and amp I play on, which is why I go the extra distance to find what amps and instruments can make even the slightest difference in upping my game. Both David and Taj were very supportive of me when I was starting out, and their music inspires me endlessly.

Over a long career in music, you've created a lot of music that will be heard for a very long time. Where do you hope to go with your music in the future?

I hope *Winter Is For Lovers* is the first in a series of lap steel based instrumental albums. I also look forward to getting back to putting pen to paper and finishing up an album with words, one that I've been working of for a long time, a very raw acoustic based record, somewhat in the vein of the album I did with my mother Ellen, called *Childhood Home.*

∞

BUD ISAACS

Bud Isaacs liked to tell people he'd played a "Briggs & Stratton" or a "Black & Decker" on sessions. In fact, it was Isaacs' 8-string, Bigsby steel guitar that introduced one of the hallmarks sounds of country music. Isaacs used the two pedals on his steel to go from an E chord to an A chord. Players had previously used pedals merely to raise or lower selected strings so that they could have access to a wider variety of chord voicings. Isaacs' innovation was to use the pedals to change chords.

Webb Pierce was one of the biggest country music stars of the 1950s despite a nasal vocal delivery and loose relationship with pitch. Pierce's thirteen singles on the Billboard charts helped him buy the guitar-shaped swimming pools and silver-dollar decorated cars he's most remembered for today.

When Pierce and songwriter Tommy Hill wrote a fairly conventional three-chord ballad called *Slowly* in 1954, they can't have imagined they were starting a revolution. Musicians and listeners alike were astounded by the liquid sound of Bud Isaacs' pedal steel fills and solo - liquid moving tones against stationary notes – a sound that would become the sound of Nashville and the signature stamp of country music. In 1984, Isaacs was inducted into the Steel Guitar Hall of Fame.

How did you get the idea to add pedals to your guitar?

I figured out this kind of tuning by listening to Bob Wills [Texas Playboys]. There were three fiddles where one would stay the same note and the others would change around it. I was trying to get that sound and I finally figured it out. Paul Bigsby, in California, built me a steel that was just what I needed. He told me it would be a long time getting it then called me in a few days and said he'd had a cancellation. He sent me one right away. Those guitars had such authority about 'em. I originally had a Gibson I'd wired up with bailing wire and coat hangers and everything else trying to get that sound.

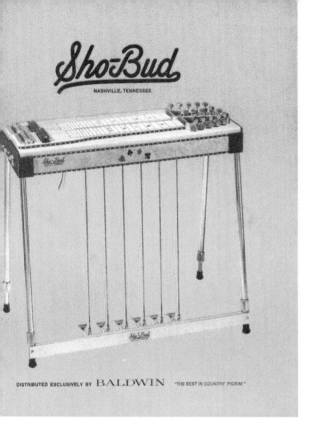

Bigsby saw it and nearly died laughing. He offered me $200 for it. I said. "What are you gonna do with it?" He said, "I'll hang it up over my shop table and whenever I need a laugh, I'll just look at that."

Was Slowly the first recording on which you used the Bigsby guitar?

I used the Bigsby on Red Foley's *Walking in the Cold Cold, Rain.* We did that before *Slowly.* I pulled a session with Web Pierce and he wanted a different sound. I had two pedals on that guitar with an E9th tuning. It was an E on top, not the Ab on top they use today. Pierce had no idea what he wanted. [Guitarist] Grady Martin said, "Listen to Budd do this intro." I done that for Webb and he said, "Okay, we'll do it that way." We didn't do sessions like you do 'em today. We just got the whole band together with one or two microphones and that was it.

Did you know the song would be a hit when you recorded it?

It was just another job to me. I never dreamed it would do what it did. It was the fastest tune to hit number one - took five days. I got pretty busy after a while. I got a lot of mail from that one from people wanting to know how it was done but they didn't dream it was foot pedals. They thought I was using a bar with camshafts. Alvino Rey played pedals long before I did but he didn't play them the same way.

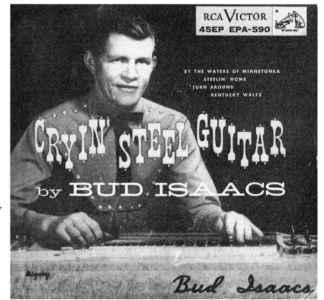

§

RAY JACKSON

To what degree does the playing of often-anonymous studio musicians contribute to making a record a hit? In the 1960s and '70s, it could often be the defining factor. The intros, hooks, fills and solos played by LA-based musicians like bassist Carol Kaye, guitarists Tommy Tedesco, Howard Roberts and Bill Pitman, drummers Earl Palmer and Hal Blaine and many others helped grease the musical wheels to transport countless hits to the top of the American charts.

In London, a smaller but no-less seasoned cadre of session aces included pianist Nicky Hopkins and guitarists Tim Renwick, Vic Flick, Ike Isaacs and even Jimmy Page, in his pre-Led Zeppelin days. Almost without exception, each of these stellar musicians played a given session on a work-for-hire basis with hardly a thought about posterity.

Does a session musician deserve additional compensation if their contribution to a given record increases its sales? In 1970, Rod Stewart was in the midst of recording his second solo album, *Every Picture Tells A Story* and having trouble finding the hook for a new song called *Maggie May*. He brought in an unknown 21 year-old mandolin player named Ray Jackson from an obscure folk-rock band called *Lindisfarne* and therein lies a story that speaks directly to this question.

After being spotted at one of Lindisfarne's first showcase gigs at London's *Marquee* club, Jackson was invited to play mandolin on a recording session produced by Elton John and Rod Stewart. His contributions were well received and, several months later, Jackson was again tapped to record with Stewart for the sessions that eventually became *Every Picture Tells A Story*.

As Jackson recalls, "The other session players had completed their parts and I was the last hired player before the album was to be mixed. I was first asked to play on *Mandolin Wind* - being the track first up on the multi track, then almost as an afterthought, *Maggie May* was played to me and I was asked to make something up from the last verse to the end of the song."

Jackson was initially unimpressed with the track. "The song had no hook or proper chorus in the conventional sense," he recalls. "It seemed long and to be going nowhere after the main vocal part, I got the impression that the track probably wouldn't make the final cut. There was no time to work out the mandolin part in advance. They basically gave me a mix in the cans and I worked out my part as it was played through. They obviously liked what I had played and asked me to multi track the parts many times over to embellish the sound."

Jackson tracked his now well-known parts on a Japanese-made Columbus, flat backed electric-acoustic mandolin he bought in 1969 and still owns today. Though thirty-eight years have elapsed since *Maggie May* was recorded, the session remains fresh in Jackson's memory. "I was linked to the desk by two AKG microphones on the floor of the studio, one being the long directional type pointing at the F- hole, the other being the wedge shaped model over the strings," he recalls. "I also remember being impressed by the sound that Mike Bobak achieved in the studio monitors. The guy had a great ear. I've never quite been able to match the same sound on any record I've played on since. Rod was in attendance behind the glass while the session was being recorded, and he watched me playing to the backing track."

Jackson had been booked as a musician-for-hire for the two tracks under the standard three-hour session contract. He walked out of the session and didn't give it much thought - at first. *Maggie May* was initially released in the U.K as the B-side of Stewart's single, *Reason To Believe* but after two weeks of airplay and travel up the charts, it was reclassified as the A-side. When the album was released, Stewart's liner notes read: "The mandolin was played by the mandolin player in Lindisfarne. The name slips my mind."

"As you can imagine, at first I was disappointed that the guy couldn't be bothered to find out my name to put on the credits,"says Jackson. "I was philosophical about it however, because he mentioned the band I played in. We had just released our first album then and it probably raised our profile. I was a virtually unknown at that time, so at the expense of my own celebrity, the band at least gained something."

Maggie May became a huge hit, simultaneously topping the UK and US charts in late 1971 as did the album, *Every Picture Tells a Story*, a feat matched only by a handful of artists like Simon and Garfunkel, the Beatles and Beyoncé .

In 2003, thirty-two years after *Maggie May* hit the charts, Ray Jackson took the unprecedented step of threatening legal action against Stewart and the song's co-composer, Martin Quittenton.

In a public statement at the time Jackson said, "I am convinced that my contribution to *Maggie May*, which occurred in the early stages of my career when I was just becoming famous for my work with Lindisfarne, was essential to the success of the record." He adds today, "All I was attempting to do was claim credit for my intellectual property, which others had profited from for over 30 years. After seeking legal advice, I was assured that I had a very good case - a case strong enough for my legal team to offer to represent me on a contingency basis." The lawsuit was never pursued and cryptically, Jackson will say only that "a change in circumstances" forced him to refrain from taking action.

 In the end, Jackson feels that his playing on *Maggie May* has had little effect on his career in music. He's recently returned to the stage after a 16-year hiatus to form a new band called *The Gathering*, with former *Hellecasters*, guitarist Jerry Donahue, Donahue's daughter Kristina, drummer Clive Bunker from *Jethro Tull*, and bassist Rick Kemp of *Steeleye Span*. Jackson handles vocals, harmonica and mandolin. *Maggie May* remains a staple of oldies format radio and is probably Rod Stewart's best known recording.

§

NATO LIMA

About 80 years ago, a family of Tabajara Indians living in the jungles of northeast Brazil were befriended by an army garrison and introduced to guitar music by one of the soldiers. The family spent the next three years following the soldiers on foot along a 3,000-mile zigzag route that eventually brought them to the city of Rio de Janiero. Along the journey, two of the brothers learned to accompany simple tribal songs on the guitar, and eventually, they began performing in the city streets for tips. After years of self study and constant touring, the brothers became classical and popular concert artists, traveling the world, appearing regularly on American television and recording almost two dozen albums for RCA. It all sounds like a fever dream from the overripe imagination of a Hollywood publicist, and yet, it's all true.

Natalicio "Nato" Moriera Lima thinks he's now about 88 years old. In the jungles of the Brazilian state of Ceará, the Tabajara Indians had no need for calendars. As one of 14 brothers, Lima was named Mussapere, which means, "Number Three". His brother, Antenor, was named Herundi, "Number Four." In the Tupi language of their tribe, Lima explains, "Jara is a warrior and Taba means, "out there" so Tabajara means, "Warrior of the Out There." Their Christian names came courtesy of two of the soldiers who befriended the tribe. As Lima recalls, "We adopted these names because they didn't know what to call us. We were Indians without education, without knowledge. They said, "We are going to call you Lima and Morena". That's how we got these names."

Lima is a man with a ready laugh and a razor-sharp memory. Just before the family encountered the soldiers, their father acquired a guitar, though none of them could play it. "They make friendship with us and we showed them the guitar we had found," he recalls, "and a soldier, he played a little bit of classical music and it was beautiful".

With a serious drought in the Northern states, Lima's father decided to follow the soldiers when they moved on. Tragedy and hardship ensued as the family moved constantly through the mountains, jungles and scrub forests for about three years. His father was briefly arrested for killing five bandits who had attacked the family and murdered Lima's aunt. And, tragically, his mother died in childbirth as she delivered their fifteenth child - and first girl. The family hunted and fished by day and slept under the stars at night. Amidst the hardships of the road, Nato and Antenor had the opportunity to see and hear guitarists playing folk music. They soon added some Brazilian songs to their repertoire of tribal chants, but other priorities came before music. "We sold that guitar for eight pounds of beans," Lima remembers.

Lacking any knowledge of the Portuguese language and unfamiliar with the concept of money, they arrived in the tropical city of Rio. There, the family saw street lights, automobiles and radios for the first time and were overwhelmed by the generosity they received. "Amazingly, the people there buy us clothes and gave us foods that we never saw before", says Lima. "The Rio de Janiero people gave us some money, and we got a new guitar. We sat on the sidewalk and we play the guitar and were singing. They threw coins to us, and it was very good."

For the next ten years, the two brothers played bars, taverns and small-town circuses in Rio and neighboring states, eventually graduating to cabarets and theaters. Fearing retribution, they hid their Indian heritage. As Lima recalls, "When we were in Rio De Janiero, one guy who managed the tour was very frustrated to discover that we were Indian because we were very afraid to say so because we were told not to say that we were Indian. But he was very smart. He found out that we were Indian and said, "I'm going to give you a contract for one week but you have to use the name of your tribe." Now outfitted in colorful native garb woven by Antenor, they began to attract attention and were asked repeatedly to tell their story to newspapers and magazines.

Throughout this period, the duo's music was limited to folk and popular songs, but that changed in 1947 when they toured South America. As Lima recalls, "We went to Chile, where we met one boy who said, "You play very good music, this Indian music. It's very beautiful, but you have to hear the most beautiful music in the world." He played them a recording of Frédéric Chopin's *Fantasie Impromptu*.

"We were completely ignorant in music," Lima says. "We couldn't even read, but we loved that music. Fantastic! We decided to play a little bit of that," says Lima. "We had good memories - photographic memories. We remembered every detail of this music. We were trying to imitate it, but this was not possible. It was not really correct, but we played a little bit of this classical music and people liked it. One club owner said, "No, no this kind of music is not liked," but the people protested and we started playing it again (*laughs*)."

It was at this point that Nato and Antenor decided on some serious woodshedding and began a rigorous study of classical guitar. Lima taught himself to read music, working night and day to understand and painstakingly adapt piano and violin music to the guitar. As Lima explains, "We decided to create a style with two guitars: one tuned high, and the other concert guitar with the sixth string tuned to low A, like the fifth string but fatter. My brother's guitar was tuned in the key of F, and my guitar was tuned one tone higher, to F#. My first string was an F#."

A further innovation came about as Lima commissioned a luthier to build him a smaller guitar with 26 frets, in place of the 19 frets usually found on a classical guitar. As Lima recalls, "Naturally, the small, very high frets are difficult to play but I did a lot to practice my technique. The high notes are very brilliant and have lots of sustain. Our highest note was a G# and the lowest note was A, on the lowest string of my brother's guitar. He learned the bass of the chords at contra tempo. He made the same bass as the piano. Sometimes Antenor played melody and

I accompanied but mostly, we alternated. Usually, I played the melody and he played the accompaniment in the bass strings. He was very good at that. The guitar has a better sound than the piano; a very round sound. If you play carefully, the guitar is the most beautiful sound in the world."

Lima developed his incredible technique on the instrument completely on his own. "I learned music by myself," he explains. "I studied all the classical methods of Albenitz, Tarrega and I learned by reading the transcriptions by Segovia. Later, I adopted my own style with the long scale guitar with extra frets. The classical guitar had a limitation of 19 frets and the velocity of the guitar is not like the violin but my technique permitted that velocity. That velocity is not easy to reach. When I played at metronome 200 [beats per minute]I used a special pick. I play the two styles because sometimes the notes are very slow, and you have to use the fingers because they are more beautiful, more velvet and more sonic. The pick is a little bit harder, but nobody noticed when we played the two styles together."

Now billed as Los Indios Tabajaras, the brothers perfected their formula throughout the 1940s with tours of South America, Spain and Europe, and they astonished audiences with their versatility. First, they played South American folk and popular melodies while dressed in Indian garb, complete with feathered headdresses. Then they'd return after intermission, dressed in tuxedos, to play music by Bach, Chopin, Tchaikovsky and other classical composers. By 1957, their manager was anxious for them to try their luck in North America but upon their arrival in New York, they couldn't get any bookings. As Lima recalls, "We didn't belong to the musicians union. It was impossible at that time to play one note anywhere without having a musician's card. We went over to the union hall but couldn't get a card. They didn't care for Indian tourist musicians so we went away, but in the elevator, we met a small, white haired guy. He said, "You come tomorrow, I'm going to give you a musician's card because I like your long hair." He was a long hair too. (*Laughs*) We got lucky that day."

Stuck in a strange country and practically broke, the brothers got a break: a chance to try to win a one-week contest on Arthur Godfrey's CBS television show. Godfrey was one of the biggest stars in the early days of television and his show, *Arthur Godfrey's Talent Scouts*, was a consistent top-ten hit. "*Talent Scouts*" presented new "discoveries" - most of whom were professionals looking for a break - to their live radio and television audience. The weekly winner was chosen by audience applause and often joined Godfrey on his shows for some time thereafter.

"We lost," Lima remembers. "We had played *Ritual Fire Dance* by Manuel De Falla. The audience liked it, but when it was time to judge the group, our applause was very small. The people started protesting. From the street, they started protesting that we were more original and we were good, playing classical music. Then Arthur Godfrey called us back, and we played 14 weeks after we lost! That was a big success."

Their appearances with Godfrey led to recording *Sweet and Savage*, an album of popular songs for RCA, and more television appearances with Ed Sullivan and Jack Paar but the album failed to generate more work. With their bookings falling off, the duo returned to Brazil. Three years later, however, RCA management called to tell them that *Maria Elena*, one of the songs on their record, was a huge hit. New York radio station WNEW had taken to playing the song between news segments and station breaks, which generated a flood of listener phone calls. RCA quickly re-released Maria Elena as a single. The brothers returned to the U.S. to an RCA recording contract and a flurry of television and concert appearances awaiting them.

While in Brazil, Lima had started playing a Brazilian-made, nylon-string resonator in addition to his standard classical guitar. That guitar, know as a Del Vecchio Dinamico, had a unique penetrating tone with unbelievably long sustain. Coupled with Lima's inimitable vibrato, it delivered a sound unlike that of any other acoustic instrument.

"Angelo Del Vecchio was my very good friend," Lima explains. "He made many 26-fret classical guitars for me. "When I came back from the United States, I said, "Make one resonator guitar for me. It was made of rosewood. It was not in tune after the 12th fret. By the 17th, 18th, 19th fret, it was almost half a step higher. Years later in the United States, we met Paul Mcgill, and McGill was the one that made those guitars have the tuning perfect. I played the McGill in Carnegie Hall for the 'Motto Perpetuo' of Pagannini, the fastest music in the world, and I now have three McGill's resonator guitars."

One guitarist who fell in love with the Del Vecchio sound after hearing Nato Lima was the great Chet Atkins. As Atkins recalled in his book, *Me and my Guitars,* "I just couldn't get over the guitar sound Nato was getting. The tone and sustain were astounding for an acoustic guitar and combined with Nato's wonderful touch, I was very impressed. I investigated, and discovered the existence of the Brazilian-made Del Vecchio resonator guitar. The Del Vecchio is a strange looking thing. The round resonator ports on the top have grille covers that make them look like built-in speakers. Combining the nylon string, classic sound with a resonating sound box produces the most impressive acoustic sound I've ever heard out of a guitar. I got in touch with Nato and began to bug him to find one for me."

Lima was accommodating. "Yes, he liked that guitar so much," he says. "I sent it to him at RCA and didn't charge anything but the RCA director said, "No, Chet wants to pay." So I sold it for a few hundred. He played a lot with that guitar. We were friends and we went every year to Nashville to play but in Nashville, they liked the popular, they don't appreciate so much the classical. When Chet passed away we didn't go anymore."

Maria Elena was a top 40 Billboard hit and Natolicio and Antenor parlayed that success into a 16-year recording career with RCA. *Maria Elena* and their album *Casually Classic* each sold more than one million copies. They appeared on the Johnny Carson show more than 20 times, and performed with symphony orchestras across the country. Lima applied his trademark vibrato to a wide range of classical music as well as the entire spectrum of pop music: *Girl from Ipanema* to Hawaiian music. "I had to practice a lot to make my vibrato natural without exaggeration because if the wave is too long, too big, it sounds bad. If it's too short, nobody notices."

In 1979, Antenor tired of the road and decided to return to Brazil to retire.

Lima brought his Japanese-born wife, Michiko, into the act to take his place, teaching her how to play the guitar from scratch. According to Marcel Ventura, their manager at the time, "They literally locked themselves in their apartment for about 15 months and practiced and practiced. It is absolutely amazing how Michiko learned so fast." The husband and wife duo continued to concertize under the *Los Indios Tabajaras* banner.

Asked which music he finds most difficult, Lima replies, *Fantasie-Impromptu* was one because in the first minute you get *tired*, the muscles don't work and you have to play all the music 'til the end without failing."
He cites *Casually Classic* as his favorite among their two dozen albums and claims he couldn't play music he doesn't like. "If you don't like it, the music has no beautiful basis and if the melody isn't original and elegant, you don't play it because you get bored. I never could like rock. It's not very complicated and besides, they don't play very well. They play badly and they make a sound that's confusing." To illustrate, he imitates the sound of a rubber band. "But the younger generation likes those things. They buy a lot of records *(laughs)."*

Despite his virtuosity, Lima also eschews jazz improvisation, preferring to stick with music that puts food on the table. "I tried a little bit but was not completely professional", he explains. "There's lots of good professionals in this kind of music but the sales are very small. If you don't sell big, I feel like it's better to play what you know or it's very expensive for you. I love this kind of jazz like Django Reinhardt, and I love the Spanish classical guitar but they are not very commercial." These days, Lima admires the work of classical guitarists David Russell and Amanda Cook.

After living in New York City for fifty years, the Limas retired to Brazil, near the city of San Paolo. "I have land there; beautiful, flat, fertile land," he explains. "I was born there. I miss the jungle. It's the most beautiful life to be in the middle of the jungle. It's very big."

One question still remains: Exactly how does Nato Lima produce his trademark vibrato, the singular sound that for 60 years has entranced listeners in 40 countries? "Hold on a minute," he replies, "I'll show you." Soon, that remarkable sound - the same sound that graced all those classic *Los Indios Tabajaras* records – comes through the lo-fi telephone speaker. But how do you describe the sound of magic?

§

TONY MOTTOLA

Elevator music. The soundtrack of the dentist's office. *Easy Listening* music doesn't get much respect from guitarists weaned on Telecaster twang or the incendiary tone of a Les Paul through a Marshall stack. But some of the best musicians have made a good living playing in the studios applying their first-call skills to the E*asy Listening genre during the 1950s and '60s.* One of the finest was guitarist Tony Mottola.

I first heard Mottola as a teenager when I picked up a bargain bin LP called *Guitar, Paris.* Alternating between electric and acoustic guitar over lush orchestral backgrounds of strings, flutes, clarinets and accordion, Mottola's jazzy lines and chord melody flourishes were recorded with an impressive, almost hyper-realism that spotlighted his warm, expressive touch and flawless phrasing. This was a guitarist to reckon with.

As I investigated, I learned that Mottola was one of the most prolific and well-respected of the studio musicians active in the New York area following World War II. Mottola had been a high school classmate of guitarists Al Cailoa and Al Viola, both masterful players and session legends. Mottola's career highlights included working in the CBS radio studio orchestra with Frank Sinatra and playing a significant role in several shows in the early days of broadcast television. These included serving as Perry Como's arranger, composing the score for the early CBS suspense anthology series, "Danger," performing in the studio bands for Sid Caesar and Mitch Miller's hit television shows and becoming one of the original members of the "Tonight Show" band.

It was Mottola's visibility on the NY scene that led producer Enoch Light to make him a mainstay of his *Command Records* label. Light was a pioneer in creating *Easy Listening* recordings that were recorded with state-of-the-art studio gear yielding exceptional sound quality – the kinds of records bachelor-pad-era Hi-Fi nerds would use to proudly demonstrate the capabilities of their latest stereo gear.

Mottola recorded more than 30 albums for the *Command* and *Project 3* labels that capitalized on his warm, tender sound and expressive phrasing on both electric and acoustic guitars. Many albums, like *Roman Guitar*, were almost cinematic in evoking a specific locale. Mottola ended his career as it had begun, working alongside Frank Sintatra, who would offer him a solo or duet showcase at his live concerts. Their working relationship continued until the guitarist's retirement in 1988. Tony Mottola died in 2004.

§

EARL "JOAQUIN" MURPHEY

The Charlie Parker of the steel guitar. That's how contemporary Western Swing steel guitar master Tom Morrell described Joaquin Murphey because, like Parker, he was a musician whose playing revolutionized his instrument and laid out a path followed by legions of musicians for many years to come. When Earl James "Joaquin" Murphey first arrived on the Los Angeles music scene of the 1940s, audiences were captivated by the swinging creativity of his improvised solos. Steel guitar players were dumbfounded. He was so far ahead of his contemporaries that it was twenty years before any other steel guitarists came close to matching the cascading jazz single note runs and chordal passages that came tumbling effortlessly out of his amplifier on a nightly basis.

Joaquin Murphey's playing combined previously unheard rhythmic and melodic invention with an ear for modern harmony delivered with astonishing technique and consummate musicality. The right hand control of Hawaiian steel pioneer Sol Hoopii, the guitar arpeggios of gypsy jazz genius Django Reinhardt, the block piano chords of George Shearing, and most importantly, the fluid clarinet runs of Benny Goodman, all found voice in the Western Swing music Murphey played with Spade Cooley, Tex Williams, Roy Rogers, Andy Parker's *Plainsmen*, and a host of other Los Angeles–based groups.

Born on December 30th, 1923, in Los Angeles, Murphey was called E.J. as a child. His introduction to the Hawaiian Steel Guitar came about when a door-to-door salesman came calling through his Hollywood neighborhood in an effort to enroll students for Hawaiian Steel Guitar lessons. His mother answered the door and after listening to the sales pitch, called E. J. to come to the door. Though he attempted an escape to the backyard, Murphey's mother would not be dissuaded – even going so far as to call his father home from work.

This was the heyday of Hawaiian music and the movie studios, radio stations and nightclubs of greater Los Angeles were a hotbed for commercialized Hawaiian music which, almost always, included the sound of the steel guitar. Murphey began lessons at Ronald Ball's (father of steel guitarist and string maker, Ernie Ball) music studio, initially using an acoustic flat-top guitar with a raised nut that allowed the Spanish guitar to be played as a steel guitar. Some of the top Hawaiian players such as Sol Hoopii and Dick McIntire spent time at Ball's studio and it wasn't long before the teenage Murphey could imitate their styles with uncanny accuracy. This early exposure to traditional Hawaiian playing is evident in Joaquin's lifelong use of smooth vibrato and the voice-like expressiveness of his playing even at breakneck tempos.

Murphey's first electric guitar was a 6-string Dickerson lap steel bought for him by his parents. This was the instrument he used to audition for the *Spade Cooley Band* in 1941, just short of his 18th birthday. Writing in the *Journal of Country Music*, Kenneth Rainey included Murphey's recollection of his audition in the kitchen of the Riverside Ranchero. "We did a couple of songs. I think the first one was 'Limehouse Blues' and that was it. Smoky (Rogers) and Tex (Williams) liked it and told Spade (Cooley) I was what they needed." This being the early years of WWII, the draft was on and opportunities arose for younger musicians that might not otherwise have been available as bands sought to replace members who had been drafted. Murphey was exempted from military service because of lung damage from double pneumonia. Cooley called the day after his audition to tell him that he and guitarist Johnny Weiss were hired.

Oklahoma-born Donnel Clyde 'Spade' Cooley was a fiddler whose band was among the hottest on the west coast, nightly filling dance halls holding thousands of people. The Cooley band was a "reading" band, working from tight arrangements penned primarily by accordionist Larry 'Pedro' DePaul, a conservatory-trained musician who also played violin and trombone. Murphey, however, had never learned to read music and had to learn his parts by ear during the band's rehearsals. Still, Murphey's prodigious musical gifts were readily apparent to his band mates and Cooley, usually a strict perfectionist, told him, "Don't worry about the melody. Just play your style. Just play around the chords, and play around the melody, 'cause we've already established the melody. Just play the way you feel." DePaul then made it a habit to leave several bars of solo space within the written arrangements for Murphey's improvisations.

Probably to better reflect the southwestern roots of their core audience, it was the band's practice to "westernize" the musicians' nicknames. Thus Illinois-born Sollie Paul Williams became 'Tex' Williams and Cooley bestowed on Murphey the life-long handle, 'Joaquin'. Despite his youth, Murphey developed into an exceptional soloist. The band was hugely popular and worked regularly at dances and on the radio. As he gained more professional experience, Murphey left his early Hawaiian influences behind and began to listen intently to jazz musicians like clarinetists Benny Goodman and Ernie Felice, guitarists Django Reinhardt and Les Paul, and later, to the British jazz pianist George Shearing, who was noted for using a "locked hands" technique to play sophisticated solos using block chords. Later in life, with tongue in cheek, Murphey told producer Michael Johnstone, "My favorite steel player is George Shearing." Outside of Noel Boggs, he claimed not to listen much to other steel guitar players.

After some time with the band on a borrowed National guitar, Murphey was approached at a dance gig by legendary Downey, California guitar maker Paul Bigsby, who offered to build him a custom steel guitar. Bigsby was a machinist by trade and a master at crafting all aspects of his instruments from their figured maple bodies to their electronics and aluminum parts. At the time, a Bigsby guitar was considered by many to be the finest custom instrument available and vintage Bigsby instruments command high prices today. Murphey's first double-8 lap Bigsby lap steel (dated 12-20-48) is now owned by luthier, musician and collector Chas Smith. Murphey eventually owned several Bigsby steels including a triple-8 with no pedals and a single-8 with six pedals.

He was also seen playing gigs in the 1950s on a double-8 Magnatone guitar. His last guitar was a custom 9-string with 4 pedals and 3 knee levers custom made by Chas Smith that included a specially designed "Bigsby-esque" pickup built by the late Danny Shields.

In 1946, Murphey and accordionist George Bamby left the Cooley band to join *Andy Parker and the Plainsmen* and later, joined vocalist Tex Williams when he took the nucleus of the Cooley band with him to form *Tex Williams and His Western Caravan*. With Murphey on board, both groups had a soloist capable of inflecting the simplest three chord song with hot jazz. Murphey was able to achieve a new level of spontaneity that hadn't been possible within the more tightly arranged Cooley band.

While many of his contemporaries spent considerable time on the road, Murphey remained in and around Los Angeles for most of the 1950s, '60s and '70s. This naturally limited his visibility, though he remained a legend to legions of awestruck steel guitarists. Feeling that the commercial E9th tuning popularized by Nashville pedal players was just a gimmick, Murphey stayed with his tunings and the non-pedal instrument long after most of his contemporaries had gone to pedal steel.

By the 1980s, Murphey had developed a life-threatening drinking problem, had his guitar repossessed and lived in a mobile home in the California desert. He hadn't touched an instrument in 13 or 14 years when musicians Chas Smith and Mike Johnstone decided to intervene. Johnstone helped him clean up. Smith builit him a new Bigsby-like pedal steel guitar and slowly, Murphey began to play again, writing songs for a new album produced in Johnstone's studio. The resulting CD, simply titled 'Murph', surrounded him with talented musicians who understood his style. It served as a showcase for a master swing musician revisiting the lush harmonies of the big band era. While his chops were diminished by time, his harmonic imagination remained staggering. Unfortunately, he did not live to see the record released. Joaquin Murphey died of cancer in 1999.

Earl James Murphey was lucky enough to be at the epicentre of Hawaiian music in America in its heyday and contributed to the flowering of west coast Western Swing. His musical influence on country music, Western Swing and on every steel guitar player who's heard him for over 50 years is incalculable.

This essay originally appreared in the book "Joaquin Murphey: Classic Western Swing Guitar Solos" by John McGann and Andy Volk.

§

CHARLES "SKIP" PITTS

Who's the cat that won't cop out when there's danger all about? The late soul singer Isaac Hayes wrote the funky theme song for *Shaft*, director Gordon Park's gritty story of a street-smart detective, and the composer's ground-breaking blend of soul and funk with traditional soundtrack orchestration helped propel the story forward. Hayes' theme song would become a huge radio hit - thanks as much to Skip Pitts' unforgettable syncopated, wah-wah pedal groove as Hayes' evocative lyrics.

Charles "Skip" Pitts had a long pedigree in rhythm and blues music before he ever put foot to pedal. He turned pro at seventeen, filling the electric guitar chair with Gene ("Duke of Earl") Chandler's band. Pitts did multiple tours with Chandler through the "Chitlin Circuit," where he rubbed shoulders with musicians like Sam and Dave, Jerry Butler, Gladys Knight and the Pips, Curtis Mayfield and the Impressions and a young, unknown guitarist named Jimi Hendrix.

"I was with Gene 'til mid '68 when our band merged with Wilson Picket's," Pitts recalls. "We didn't record with Gene, because Atlantic was using Steve Cropper and the Muscle Shoals guys in the studio. I played with Picket's tour band, the Midnight Movers. I got my first wah wah pedal while I was with Pickett in '68 or early '69. My first wife knew Isaac Hayes and he told her he was looking for a guitar player." Pitts jammed with Hayes and was hired on the spot.

In 1971, Gordon Parks tapped Hayes to work on his upcoming movie. As Pitts recalls, "We were working on the score at MGM in Culiver City. I had a Maestro Boomerang wah-wah and a Gibson Les Paul guitar. I was testing my wah-wah and all my foot pedals and I was hitting a rhythm with that pedal and trying to keep that going. Isaac wrote the song around that part after we got it down on tape. He told [drummer] Willy Hall that he wanted something moving - like a sixteenth note rhythm. He asked me to add onto the flavor of what Willy was doing. We were looking at the footage the whole time we worked on the movie. That's why the count is so off in certain parts. We had to make it fit the footage."

Asked if he thought the tune was a hit, Pitts replies emphatically, "Hell no! Everyone was listening to the playback on *Shaft* before we moved on. Gordon Parks, Hayes and all of them were making a big hoopla over what I was doing and I didn't understand it because to me, what I had played was simple. I'm not going to say I didn't dig it but I had no idea what it would turn out to be. If I'd known that, I'd have asked for half writer's credit," he laughs.

The *Theme from Shaft* was a huge hit for Hayes and reinvigorated his career. Pitts remained a member of Hayes' band throughout the 1970s and was his guitarist and bandleader at the time of Hayes' death in August 2008 - this despite a rift between the two spurred by an interview with *Blender Magazine* where Hayes described how he had gotten down on his knees to operate Pitts' wah-wah pedal by hand to create the famous part.

"I was furious when I read that," says Pitts, "but I didn't want to approach Isaac at that time because Isaac had just had a stroke. No, he didn't get down on his hands and knees to operate the wah wah. How in the world could you do that? It's ridiculous. Guitar players can hardly do it! I was playing wah wah back when I was with the Isley Brothers. If you listen to their album with *It's Your Thing [1969]*, you can hear some wah-wah things I did that sound like *Shaft*. I got with Isaac in '70."

Despite this bump in the friendship, Pitts remains loyal to Hayes' memory. "He was my buddy," explains Pitts. "Other than that statement about the wah-wah, he's been pretty straight up about how things happened. This is history - the first Blaxploitation film, the first black Academy Award!"

Pitts revived the theme one more time in the year 2000 with a crew of New York studio musicians for the score of the Samuel Jackson remake of Shaft. "I'm playing today with a group called the Bo-Keys," says Pitts. As he puts it, "We're bringing back all the old guys who are still kicking ass!"

§

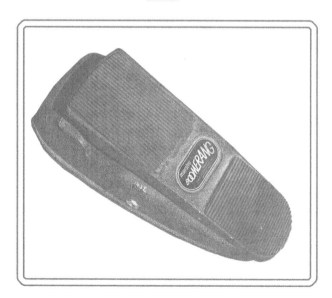

ELLIOTT RANDALL

Steely Dan's chart-topping 1972 debut album, *Can't Buy A Thrill*, set a new watermark for harmonically and melodically sophisticated rock that introduced a new breed of studio sideman, players like Larry Carlton and Elliott Randall who understood jazz but could deliver a rock hook with scary authority. Randall's virtuoso Celtic-meets-rock performance on Reelin' in the Years (the first single released from the LP) has been a perennial favourite on many lists of the all-time best solos in rock & roll.

While best known for that seminal performance thirty-seven years ago, Randall has enjoyed a long just-below-the-radar career that started in the early 1960s backing vocal groups - like The Ronnettes and The Capris. Besides Steely Dan, he's shared the studio with a dizzyingly diverse group of artists including Carly Simon, Peter Frampton, The Doobie Brothers, Jimmy Webb, Joan Baez, Liza Minelli, and The Rochester Philharmonic, as well as composed and performed on hundreds of commercials, film, and television projects.

His connections in the 1960s New York studio scene led to a friendship with future Steely Dan founders, Donald Fagen and Walter Becker. When Randall left New York for California in 1972, he reunited with them and his childhood friend, Jeff "Skunk" Baxter, when they invited him to work on *Can't Buy a Thrill*.

Since the early 1980s, Randall's had a side career as a consultant on instrument and amplifier design, recording and sampling technology, software design, and music education for companies like Roland, Korg and Yamaha. Yet despite these credentials, he's probably best known in the guitar community for his indelible performance on *Reelin' in the Years*. I was interested in learning how that solo came to be and the effect it's had on Randall's career.

Your intro and guitar solo on Reelin' In The Years is widely considered as one of the all-time great rock guitar performances. How did you come to be hired to play on the session?

Donald, Walter and I go back to pre-Steely Dan days, when we were all back-up musicians for a vocal group called Jay & The Americans. One of the group, a fellow called Kenny Vance, saw the talent these guys possessed as writers, and produced a plethora of demo recordings in a small New York recording studio called Mayfair Sound. I played on many of these.

When they relocated to LA and formed a band, they asked if I would play on some of the tunes for their first record for ABC-Dunhill. At that time, I declined their invitation to join the group full time, which led to me playing on several of their later albums, after the original 'group' was 'no more'.

How did the song evolve and what instructions were you given about what to play?

On the evening that I came in to overdub the leads on *Reelin'*, they simply said, "do your thing" – not another word, really. It was 100 percent 'off the cuff'. When it comes to soloing, I find it much more enjoyable to be given the opportunity to go wherever the spirit takes me, but on the other hand, I've had to learn and play certain written solos for orchestral pieces in the past; also an enjoyable experience.

What guitar, amp, effects, etc. did you use?

Oh, if I had ten bucks for every time I've been asked that question, I could probably put triplets through college! The ingredients were: my '63 Fender Stratocaster, using the neck pickup, which was a '69 Gibson PAF and the only amp that was in the studio that night - an Ampeg SVT – a beast of an amp that I certainly wouldn't have picked, if I'd had a choice. But we cranked it up to 11, Roger Nichols hunted around for the sweet spot to place his mic, found it, and voilà!

You've been a working musician, bandleader and producer for many years, collaborating with hundreds of great artists. Are you asked about "Reelin' in the Years" often? How does it feel to be so identified by a single solo you played over thirty years ago?

How can I possibly complain? Needless to say it's always gratifying when someone appreciates my work and so it never ends - the quest for the lost chord! The Steely Dan connection has always been a fun one. I can't remember ever having a bad time when making music with them.

Has playing on the record helped or hindered your career?

Back in the '70s when it first hit the radio, the demand for my services in the recording studios went through the roof. The big trick of course, is sustaining it all; the abilities, sensibilities, and 'au-currant-ness' to keep that 'demand' up. My career has blossomed into numerous other sectors of the music industry over these many years, but the call to come in and play on a quality session is still one of the most satisfying and exciting experiences for me.

You've been a producer as well as a bandleader and session musician. Which is easier/more enjoyable and why?

I'll try to address 'easier' part - playing one's instrument. Over time, an instrumentalist's abilities, repertoire of techniques and styles blossoms, and playing in an ensemble feels easy, fun, spiritual even – or any combo of those, depending on the circumstances. Being a bandleader and/or producer requires a completely different set

of skills. In addition to the musical skills, you need a large palette of interpersonal skills.

It's not just about dealing with other people, but getting what you need from them, and having them walk away happy with the interactions, and be wanting to deliver more and better next time. Whew! As to which is more enjoyable, in a few words: they all bring me incredible satisfaction and joy. There are always new projects happening and most of them involve recording. I'm now compiling my *Guitar Archives Volume 2* CD, which has some pretty cool and unusual performances by Blues Brother John Belushi, The Doobie Brothers [the 1979 contingent], and some other serious notables. It'll be a fun disk.

As for the guitar-for-hire part of me, a large portion of my recording is done via the Internet these days. I'd much rather be in a room full of great musicians, all playing and grooving together but at this technological place in time, that seems to be the exception rather than the rule. When I produce, I do it the good old fashioned way - all players at once, in a great studio!

§

LOUIE SHELTON

When nine year-old Louie Shelton received a $13 Stella for his birthday in 1951, he couldn't guess that the instrument would take him out of Arkansas and carry him through a lifetime career in the music business as a musician, producer and session ace on a slew of hit records.

Shelton was a natural on the guitar. Turning pro at age twelve and still in school, he played guitar with the Dixie Mountaineers' on their live gigs and weekly radio performances as well as a live television performance each Wednesday on KATV, one of Arkansas' earliest stations.

He played in a number of bands, meeting important early contacts like Memphis session legend Reggie Young, who introduced him to the recordings of jazz masters like Barney Kessel and Johnny Smith. Before long, Shelton was proficient in a range of styles across genres – the perfect background for a studio player. He gigged around the Southwest for a few years then decided to try his luck in Los Angeles. He'd met fellow Arkansas native Glen Campbell a few years earlier when they both played local clubs in Albuquerque, so Campbell was the first person Shelton he called when he arrived in California.

Few producers were willing to risk hiring an unknown player for their sessions, despite Campbell's endorsement, so, while Shelton struggled to find demo sessions he began backing artists on live gigs - like Mama Cass, Joe and Eddie, and Tiny Tim. One of the bands Louie played with included Joe Bogan, Jim Seals and Dash Crofts, later to record a string of hits as Seals & Crofts with Shelton in the producer's chair.

The LA studio doors finally opened – and stayed open – for Shelton when he was invited to play on the Monkees early records, contributing indelible licks, solos and hooks for a string of Monkees hits including *Last Train to Clarksville* and *Valerie*.

For the next twenty years, Shelton played sessions for artists including Barbara Streisand, Michael Jackson, Neil Diamond, The Carpenters, The Mamas & Papas, Ella Fitzgerald, Lionel Ritchie, John Lennon, Joe Cocker, Simon & Garfunkel, Whitney Houston, Kenny Rogers, and many, many more.

He and his family moved to Australia in 1984, opening a recording studio and producing a number of bands. Despite a return to the states for a stint in Nashville, Shelton missed Australia and decided to return there where he is still active as a musician and producer living on Australia's Gold Coast.

"After playing club gigs six nights a week from Arkansas to Santa Fe, Denver and many places in between, when I first arrived in Los Angeles my goal was to become a session guitarist. For the first couple of years I had to play club gigs and struggled just to land a few demo sessions. Tommy Boyce and Bobby Hart used me to play on all of their demo's. I had taken a gig at the Stardust Hotel in Las Vegas with a group which included Jim Seals and Dash Crofts later known as Seals & Crofts. One night Boyce and Hart showed up at our show to tell me they had landed this great opportunity to write the songs for a show, *The Monkees*, and would I come play on the recordings? Without hesitation I said yes and gave my notice to the band.

On arriving back in LA, they set up a rehearsal to try and come up with some musical ideas for the theme for *The Monkees* show and hopefully, their first single. That's where I came up with the riff and solo for *Last Train to Clarksville*, which became their first #1 single.

At some point later, as we had moved on into the recording other material, the song *Valerie* came up," Shelton recalls. "We'd recorded a couple of other songs that day and were starting to feel at home in the studio. After Tommy played a bit of Valerie on the acoustic guitar for us, we began to run the tune with the band. I started this ridiculous flamenco thing as a joke and Tommy immediately stopped and said, "That's great, remember that lick." So that's how that whole thing came about. I've had many comments about that solo. I've even heard it on a rap record. The solo was really just improvised on the spot. I was using a '60s Fender Tele through a Super Reverb amp with no effects, just cranked a bit."

As actors, the Monkees had to be on the set very early every day. They'd drag themselves into the recording studio in the evening to do their vocals after filming all day. "They were hired mainly for their acting and were not known to be great musicians or songwriters", says Shelton. "But all things considered, they could play pretty well and I thought their singing was perfect for those songs. I still get out and play live once in a while. Whenever I do a set that features some of the classic hits I played on I'm always amazed at the response. I do tunes like *Lowdown, Summer Breeze, Hello,* and *I Want You Back,* but as soon as I start the intro to "*Last Train to Clarksville*" the audience really freaks out. It's like they've been listening to that song for all these years and to see the guy who actually played it just freaks them out. That particular song really launched my session career. Sometimes, I feel people respond to it more now than when it was out years ago."

Shelton is happy and grateful to be identified with all those 60s and 70s hits. "I've only had praise from other musicians and people who are familiar with those songs," he says. "Not to be a stick in the mud, but I don't hear a lot of stuff today that people will still be listening to 40 years from now. Today I'm a producer, bandleader, session musician, engineer, arranger, recording artist, songwriter and live performer. I really enjoy all of it but my guitar playing in the studio or live is what I enjoy the most. It still feels like a hobby, but I owe all of my success to my guitar."

§

JOHNNY SMITH

"AN EXTRAORDINARY VIRTUOSO. AS FAR AS I'M CONCERNED, NO ONE IN THE WORLD PLAYS THE GUITAR BETTER THAN HE. THEY MIGHT PLAY IT DIFFERENTLY, BUT NOBODY PLAYS BETTER." - BARNEY KESSEL

Romantic. Vibrant. Shimmering. Guitarist Johnny Smith's 1952 recording with saxophonist Stan Getz of "Moonlight in Vermont" first introduced listeners to this unmatched fretboard artist. On this LP, Smith, played with effortless technical precision and stunning musicality, conjuring up an almost cinematic experience of the song's lyrics for the listener.

Harmonically speaking, the chord voicings Smith used were made up of closed-voiced intervals, notes that are physicaly close together on a piano keyboard and easy to play, but require wide stretches to finger on a guitar. Over his long career, Smith arranged many beautiful chord melody treatments in this style for both standard tunes and classical piece's like Debussy's "Girl with the Flaxen Hair", as well as traditional folk songs such as "Shenandoah" and "Black is the Color of My True Love's Hair." These challenging, timeless arrangements have inspired guitarists for more than sixty years.

Meticulous in his musicianship, Smith was superhumanly smooth, clean and precise in his execution, capable of playing three octave arpeggios at astonishing speed. This level of virtuosity enabled him to explore the guitar in ways that were in some ways closer to a virtuoso classical pianist than a blues influenced jazz musician. While this level of technique and sophistication was initially novel and intoxicating to his fellow jazz guitarists in the early 1950s, the impression that ultimately lingered was that his technique was completely at the service of a breathtaking musical art. Despite his utter mastery of the jazz idiom, Smith emphatically maintained that he didn't consider himself to be a jazz guitarist.

Born in Birmingham, Alabama in 1922, John Henry Smith, Jr. grew up in Portland, Maine. As a teenager, he made a deal with a local pawnshop: he'd keep the store's guitars in tune if he could use them to teach himself to play. In little time, he was teaching others and playing country music doing gigs all over Maine for $4 a night with Uncle Lem and the Mountain Boys. Meanwhile, Smith was absorbing the music of Django Reinhardt and the arranging techniques of the big band music that was ubiquitous on the radio. During WWII, Smith used his time in the military marching band to learn to read music from trumpet and violin instruction books. After the war, Smith returned to Portland playing nightclub gigs and a daily radio show on guitar and trumpet in a pit band. It wasn't long before New York beckoned. "The three networks, NBC, ABC, and CBS, each had over 100 musicians on full-time staff. Everything was live music, right down to the commercials, and it was wonderful. And, of course, 52nd Street was door-to-door-to-door jazz. Then there was Birdland." Recalled Smith. "I feel fortunate and grateful to have been there."

"WHEN HE FIRST CAME TO NEW YORK HE SCARED EVERY GUITAR PLAYER TO DEATH."
- BUCKY PIZZARELLI

Smith was equally at home play jazz gigs with his trio, sight-reading scores in the orchestra pit of the New York Philharmonic, or serving as a studio guitarist and arranger for NBC, a job he filled from 1946 to 1958. In any given week, Smith played in a variety of settings from backing vocalists, to solo and trio performances, to gigs with a full orchestra. He became possibly the most admired guitar player on the New York jazz scene during the 1950s, often playing opposite legendary jazz figures such as Charlie Parker, Dizzy Gillespie, Count Basie, Lester Young, Miles Davis, Billie Holiday, and Art Tatum.

Throughout the 1950s, at the same time he was setting new standards for chord melody guitar, Smith released album after album of straight ahead, single note jazz guitar playing in group settings that was notable for its clarity, flow and light swing feeling.

The salient features of his approach stayed the same for his entire career. In addition to his facility with chord melody, as a single note player, Smith largely eschewed the chromatically-based language of be-bop in favor of a largely diatonic, non-blues-based style.

Ironically, Smith's best known musical composition is "Walk Don't Run" (based on the chord progression of "Softly, as in a Morning Sunrise") recorded in 1954. It's fame was almost entirely due to the 1960 version recorded by instrumental rock legends "The Ventures", whose version stayed at No. 2 on the Billboard Top 100 for a week and is still played today.

As meticulous as he was about his playing, Smith was equally precise about stringing and tuning his instruments. In 1984, he told Guitar Player Magazine, "Those of us who fly light twin-engine airplanes use the [differential] wave to synchronize the RPM of the two propellers. If you want to make your passengers uncomfortable, fly with the props out of synch. By the same token, if you want to make an audience uncomfortable, play with out-of-tune instruments."

Besides his innovations as a player, Smith was also involved in guitar and amplifier design for Epiphone, Gibson and D'Angelico and Ampeg These relationships were sometimes a bit rocky. As Smith recalled, His first D'Angelico met an unfortunate end. "When I heard about John D'Angelico, he made me a guitar that was absolutely beautiful. But the house I was renting on Long Island burned down and, unfortunately, took my guitar and my dog.", he recalled.

Besides his innovations as a player, Smith was also involved in guitar and amplifier design for Epiphone, Gibson and DeAngelico and Ampeg. These relationships were sometimes a bit rocky. As Smith recalled, His first DAngelico met an unfortunate end. "When I heard about John D'Angelico, he made me a guitar that was absolutely beautiful. But the house I was renting on Long Island burned down and, unfortunately, took my guitar and my dog.", he recalled.

Smith accepted a design contract with Gibson but refused their prototype Signature Model because it had 22 frets. Like his D'Angelicos, Smith wanted only 20 frets both to facilitate his playing style, which employed long stretches, and to create an overall more mellow tone." He also worked with Everett Hull to design Ampeg's "Fountain of Sound" amplifier which eventually became a mainstay of the New York studio scene. Inspired by the upwardly bent bell of Dizzy Gillespie's horn, the amp's speakers were aimed skyward. As Smith remembered, "It kept the sound out of people's ears, because in those days, people complained when things were too loud."

He also worked with Everett Hull to design Ampeg's "Fountain of Sound" amplifier which eventually became a mainstay of the New York studio scene. Inspired by the upwardly bent bell of Dizzy Gillespie's horn, the amp's speakers were aimed skyward. As Smith remembered, "It kept the sound out of people's ears, because in those days, people complained when things were too loud." His Signature Gibson Sonomatic string set was also non standard. It came with a flat wound low E string because he so often tuned that string down from E to D.

In the modern era, Guild, Gibson, Heritage, and Benedetto all have signature Johnny Smith signature models in tribute to Smith's stature as player and insightful consultant on instrument design.

Tragically, in 1957, Smith's wife and second child died in childbirth. He sent his young daughter to Colorado Springs, Colorado to be with his mother, and in 1958, he left his busy performing career in New York City to join his daughter there.

As quoted in his New York Times obituary, Smith said, "In the end, everything came down to the fact that I loved my daughter too much to let my career put her at risk. But there were other factors, too. I loved New York musically, but I hated living there."

Smith ran a musical instruments store in Colorado Springs, taught music, and raised his daughter while continuing to record solo and group albums for jazz labels like Verve and Royal Roost. A perfectionist to the core, Smith had a reputation for being unhappy with his recordings. According to Smith, "The truth is, the minute you record something, you look back and realize you could have done it better."

By 2013, when he died at age 91, few guitarists were as universally revered and admired as Johnny Smith, yet he always remained sincerely humble and unassuming about his extraordinary career and its impact on listeners and musicians alike. Guitarists as diverse as Bill Frisell, Larry Coryell, Ted Greene and Ry Cooder – to name a few out of thousands - all name Smith as a seminal influence. Today, his music remains the gold standard for plectrum technique and a beacon of musical excellence on the guitar.

§

GABOR SZABO

Those clanging open string dissonances; mesmerizing tunes that seamlessly combine Indian and Gypsy elements with the vocabulary of modern jazz guitar – once heard, rarely forgotten. The metallic, droning tone of Szabo's Gypsy-inflected picking on a Martin dreadnaught outfitted with a DeArmond pickup remains unique and inimitable.

Today, it's commonplace for adventurous musicians to collaborate with artists from other cultures or incorporate musical elements from various world music traditions into their recordings and live performances. Paul Simon, Ry Cooder, Pierre Bensusan, Martin Simpson, and Bob Brozman are just a few of the more visible guitarists noted for their collaborations with musicians from Algeria, Africa, Brazil, China, Cuba, Hawaii, New Guinea, Okinawa, and other locations around the globe.

If flavoring one's musical stew with multi-cultural elements is almost de rigueur today, it was certainly out-of-the-box thinking in the early 1960s - especially in jazz. Even though Dizzy Gillespie had incorporated Cuban rhythms and rhythm sections into bebop as early as the 1940s, it took the sense of exploration and widespread chaffing against social and artistic barriers of the 1960s to truly open the pan-national floodgates. Long before "world music" became it's own category, Gabor Szabo was among the first to demonstrate the creative power of fusing world music elements with jazz, rock, raga, pop and even electronic feedback.

Born in Budapest, Hungary, in 1936, Szabo first developed an interest in the guitar at age 14 after seeing Roy Rogers in a movie. Thanks to Voice of America radio programs, he regularly heard jazz guitarists like Johnny Smith and Tal Farlow. He managed to slip out just ahead of the 1956 communist revolution, eventually settling in Los Angeles.

Four years at Boston's Berklee College of Music helped him forge lifelong connections with many musicians who were soon to make their mark in jazz. Initially, Szabo struggled, taking jobs as a janitor and a property manager before landing a spot in Chico Hamilton's innovative quintet. The group quickly developed a following for their unique blend of Charles Lloyd's Coltrane-influenced tenor saxophone, Szabo's Gypsy-influenced melodic guitar and Hamilton's virtuoso percussion solos. Hamilton encouraged Szabo to develop his own voice on the guitar and increasingly, Szabo incorporated the eastern European sounds of his upbringing into his music.

Gypsy 66 was Szabo's debut as a leader. That same year, he joined bassist Ron Carter and Hamilton in the studio to record *Spellbinder*, widely regarded as his best recording. The album featured an exciting array of standards, originals, and covers, including Sinatra's *It was A Very Good Year* and the Sonny & Cher, hit, *Bang Bang*. Anchored by bass and congas, the extended dominant chord vamp of the title track showcased Szabo's ability to create and sustain a mood with mesmerizing results. The album also yielded a large royalty payment in 1970 when Carlos Santana merged Szabo's composition, "Gypsy Queen" into his hit single, "Black Magic Woman." Szabo remained a seminal influence on Santana and later, became a close friend.

Interested in Indian music for many years, Szabo was now also listening intently to guitarists who were making new sounds in rock. While uneven in quality, his later '60s recordings proved his willingness to experiment as he juggled fuzz and feedback with Gypsy, jazz and pop sounds. Inspired by an attempt to mimic the sitar's drone, Szabos use of feedback was much different than Jimi Hendrix's explosive style. In Szabo's hands, electronic feedback offered a subtle way to color the music rather than dominate it.

Szabo's most influential group was his 1967 quintet with the talented classical and jazz guitarist, Jimmy Stewart. Stewart's subtle rhythm work and graceful soloing perfectly complimented Szabo's more exotic approach. Recorded live in a Boston club, *The Sorcerer* presents the group in full flight and includes Szabo's best version of his striking original composition, *Mizrab*.

Despite recording frequently during the 1970s and 80s, Szabo's music failed to generate the critical sparks of his earlier work. A heroin habit, ill health, divorce, and a deepening involvement with L. Ron Hubbard's Church of Scientology seemed to sap his work of much of its vitality. Szabo died of complications from a liver ailment on a 1981 return visit to Hungary. Though little remembered or acknowledged by today's guitarists, Szabo was nevertheless a world music fusion pioneer and a guitarist with a unique and compelling six-string voice.

§

BILL TAPIA

When Bill "Tappy" Tapia died in 2011 at age 103 he may well have held the record as be the oldest working musician in America. At an age when most people have faded into history, Tappy was busy booking gigs.

Born in Honolulu in 1908, Tapia was weaned on traditional Hawaiian music, starting on ukulele and turning pro at the mind-boggling age of twelve, when his parents took him out of school to play ukulele in a vaudeville show.

"Then when I was about 15 or 16, I got a job on a ship playing Hawaiian music with Andy Iona", explains Tapia. "I played with Andy, Solomon Hoʻopiʻi, Solomon Bright, Sam Koki and all those guys. In those days, they were the top [Hawaiian] musicians. I worked on ships going from Honolulu to San Francisco and Los Angeles. After 1935, I never played Hawaiian music anymore. I loved Jazz so I broke away from those [Hawaiian] guys and played with the best jazz players in the country."

While supplementing his income giving uke lessons to top Hollywood stars like Shirley Temple, Janet Gaynor, Jimmy Durante, and Loretta Young, Tapia changed his focus to jazz guitar. "Gibson, Gretsch or Epiphone – I had them all", he says. "My picture was in Gibson Magazine and Epiphone's catalog in the 30s. American Epiphone and Gibson were head-to-head, like a Cadillac and a Lincoln Continental - about equal. They were the best guitars. I was lucky, I wasn't the best player in the world but I could play most anything and hold my own playing with anybody. I had an eighteen-piece band in Honolulu and I worked all through WWII, playing in blackout ballrooms.

As Tapia's skills on jazz guitar became known, he worked with many of the greatest names in the music business like Bing Crosby, Charlie Barnet, and Louie Armstrong. "Louie happened to be in LA and he was my idol. So I was workin' at the Beverly Wilshire Hotel and I saw in the paper that Louie Armstrong was playing and I said, "I've gotta see this guy." I went there and I asked him if I could sit in with his band. He said, "Are you familiar with what we do?" I said, "Yeah, I think I can play anything you got." So I sat in and we became friends."

Asked if he's nostalgic for the golden age of jazz, Tapia replies, "In those days, when you played music, a musician was making two or three times more money than a finish carpenter or bricklayer. People would look at you like you wore a badge; they'd respect you. Today, it's gone to hell. You don't get respected. You did, in my day. Music was a top thing, you know? It was like being a doctor when you were a musician. I hope those days come back again."

Tapia's passion for the ukulele was rekindled a few years ago after the deaths of his daughter, Cleo, and Barbie, his wife of 62 years. Suffering from depression, Tapia again picked up the instrument and urbane jazz guitar licks soon gave way to the sweet Hawaiian sounds of his boyhood. As Tapia explains, "The ukulele was the first instrument that I learned then I didn't touch it for 56 years! Then four and a half or five years ago, everybody started going crazy for the uke. I picked one up again and never forgot what I used to do and I've been playing it all over the country. Right after this next concert, I go to San Francisco to play at Stanford University and three other gigs then on to Washington for three concerts. I'm still working, thank God."

Is Bill Tapia the oldest, still gigging musician in America? "Well, this is what they say but I don't know. I've been a musician all my life", he says. "I've been to the union. They don't know of anybody that's playing professionally at my age."

§

ERIC WEISSBERG

The scene is iconic in American film: at a gas station somewhere in the scrub-pine, three-Xs-on-the moonshine bottle, hillbilly backwoods of writer James Dickey's imagination we see an impromptu jam session unfold between an unlikely pair. The boy's banjo echoes each halting, walking-on-eggshells phrase from the guitar. Their duet builds exquisite tension before finally giving way to a joyous, rollicking cascade of Skruggs-style banjo rolls and galloping flattop guitar runs. Released in 1973 by Warner Brothers as *Dueling Banjos*, the tune became a top-selling Grammy-winning single and somewhat of an albatross around the neck of Eric Weissberg, the formerly anonymous studio musician who played banjo on the song.

For almost fifty years, Weissberg was a fixture of the New York studio scene and a legendary sideman to the best American folk performers since the late 1950s. Weissberg grew up in Greenwich Village, where he started on banjo, guitar, and violin before age ten, eventually attending Juilliard as a bass major. He taught himself bluegrass banjo by slowing down his father's 78-rpm records, further honing his chops as a co-founder of the bluegrass trio, *The Greenbriar Boys*. In 1959, Weissberg joined the folk group *The Tarriers*, recording and touring worldwide with them for six years.

Weissberg played guitar, pedal steel, mandolin, resophonic guitar, fiddle and banjo on over six thousand jingles, movie soundtracks, and record dates with Bob Dylan, Barbra Streisand, John Denver, Willie Nelson, Johnny Cash, Arlo Gutherie, The Talking Heads, Bruce Springsteen, Doc Watson, Judy Collins, Bette Midler, Buddy Rich, Jim Croce, Rick Danko and many others. When Weissberg first entered the New York studios scene, it was populated by veterans of the big band era. As folk and roots music gained greater visibility and commercial viability, Weissberg's multi-instrumental prowess filled a growing niche.

As Weissberg explains, "I began doing sessions on bass in the mid 50s while I was still in high school. The folk music thing was just catching on and I was one of the few people who knew folk music well, could read music and play the bass as well as all the folk instruments. I just kind of fit in." "Tony Mottola, Al Caiola, Don Arnone and Barry Galbraith didn't play banjo," he recalls. "When I was breaking in, those were the top guys. They did play *tenor* banjo but not five-string and, if they played mandolin, it was mainly to play Italian-sounding things. I played on several albums with Al Caiola and Tony Mottola. Those guys were all so nice to me. Don Arnone was one of the funniest guys on the planet and they were all incredible, mind-blowing guitar players but they were amazed at the fingerpicking style I was playing."

One of those wide-eyed pros was the great Belgian guitarist and harmonica virtuoso, Toots Thielmans. Playing mostly guitar in the studios at that time, Thielmans asked Weissberg to teach him Merle Travis-style alternating bass fingerstyle guitar. "He heard me doing that and his eyes were like saucers," says Weissberg. "I just showed him the rudiments of the style and a couple of weeks later we were doing another session and Toots said, "Hey, listen to this." He started playing *When My Sugar Walks Down the Street* using chords that I would never have thought to use. He's an awesome guy and an incredible musician. I'm really thankful for how nice they all were to me. Those days of my life were tremendous and kind of dreamlike, really. I was just there in the right place and time and I could do what they needed me to do."

While Weissberg still plays occasional studio dates, he laments that the scene is nothing like it was in its heyday in the 1950s through 70s when he played fifteen to twenty sessions a week, totaling four or five hundred studio gigs each year. "Including the Latin guys, there were maybe three or four hundred of us studio guys. It was kind of an elite group," he says. "And now, the elite, upper echelon of musicians working in NYC are playing Broadway shows, something I didn't enjoy doing. It was the same thing for 3000 performances."

Weissberg would likely have remained one of the legions of well-compensated but anonymous session cats had he not received a phone call in 1972 from the production coordinator for a new movie to be directed by John Boorman. Based on James Dickey's novel, *Deliverance,* the film would explore the harrowing tale of four suburbanites who get much more than they bargained for during a weekend of white water canoeing in Dickey's harrowing version of Appalachia.

As Weissberg recalls, "He said, "Do you know *Dueling Banjos*?" I said, "I know what tune you're talking about. The original tune from 1958 was called *Feudin' Banjo*s. It was Arthur Smith with one of my idols, Don Reno, and a rhythm section. [*The tune was written in 1955 and first appeared on Smith's LP, Battling Banjos*]. My dad came home with it one day and I didn't like it 'cause it wasn't really Bluegrassy so I kind of put it way and forgot about it. Carl Story did a version called *Mocking Banjo* with a tenor banjo and 5-string banjo and the Dillards also did a version *[Back porch Bluegrass, 1963]* with a banjo feuding with a mandolin player." Weissberg called his friend, Steve Mandell, to come up to the production coordinator's apartment to audition. After auditioning the tune at multiple tempos in different keys he decided he liked what he heard and asked Weissberg and Mandell to join the crew on location in Georgia.

"John Boorman wanted to film the scene and then cut it to the music, so he wanted us there to rehearse with the actors," says Weissberg. "Boorman explained that he wanted us to play slowly and tentatively because the two characters in the film were just meeting for the first time. So we worked on it for a day and a half. We did it a few different ways; slightly different each time, and we went back to Atlanta with the editor who was the producer for the music in the scene." Mandell and Weissberg were at their hotel packing up to leave when they received a call that Boorman was thrilled with the music they'd played and wanted them to stay and do cues for the rest of the movie. They flew back to New York to honor their studio gigs then cleared their calendars to return to Georgia.

"We looked at a hundred or more slightly different takes of various scenes," recalls Weissberg. "The editor would say, "We have a scene now where they're floating down the river and it lasts for about 30 seconds." So we would play something and he'd say, "Can you do a little slower or a little faster next time?" "At the end of the weekend Steve and I went back in New York and I forgot about the whole thing. I was really busy in the studios and it just went out of my mind." Weissberg was recording a jingle one day when one of the singers told him he'd heard him on the radio. Nonplussed, Weissberg learned that Warner Brothers had released some 45 rpm records of *Dueling Banjos* solely for disc jockeys to play behind promo announcements for *Deliverance* and that multiple listener phone calls had convinced the label to release a single. Released in 1973 by Warner Brothers as *Dueling Banjos,* the tune became a top-seller, eventually winning a Grammy award.

"We were watching this thing go up the charts," recalls Weissberg. "The record labels didn't have my name or Steve's name on it so I got a lawyer and it got sorted out. Then, I got the idea that Steve and I could go into the studio with a New York bluegrass band, cut twelve more sides and mix and master an album. So I was sitting across the desk from my lawyer who called Warner Brothers. He said, "I'm sitting here with Eric Weissberg and he says he can do an album in just a couple of days." Suddenly, he stopped talking and his eyes got wider and wider. He put his hand over the mouthpiece, leaned over and said, "The album's already out."

Back in 1963, Weissberg and Marshall Brickman (who later shared an Academy Award with Woody Allen for co-writing *Annie Hall)* had recorded an album for Electra called *New Dimensions in Banjo and Bluegrass.* In the ensuing 10 years, Warner Brothers had acquired Electra and the *New Dimensions* album. They removed two of Weissberg and Brickman's originals replacing them with the cuts from the *Dueling Banjos* 45.

"They did this without asking us or even telling us this what we're doing", a still annoyed, Weissberg recalls, "Our album now had a new cover and no liner notes and Marshall's great liner notes were cut out. He had covered who's playing banjo on which cuts, where's there's a double banjo, and who's playing the first break and the second break. All that was now completely gone. The only thing left was the titles of the tunes. All these decades have gone by without getting royalties for the two tunes we wrote which still really pisses me off. Most people think I played all the banjos on that record and I didn't. Marshall really hasn't gotten proper credit for decades because of the repackaging as music from *Deliverance*."

Arthur [Guitar Boogie] Smith, the composer of *Feudin' Banjo*s successfully sued Warner Brothers for credit and back royalties and, well into the internet age, Weissberg was forced to explain that he had no part in trying to cheat Smith, Bill Monroe and other writers out of their well-deserved royalties for their tunes from the *New Dimensions* LP that were included on the *Deliverance* soundtrack.

These days, Weissberg is philosophical. "We did a good job of playing it but it wasn't meant to be a record, just a background thing for a movie, so we didn't take that much care to make it absolutely perfect. I'm still glad I did it," he says. "It was just a straight-ahead bluegrass tune, not my favorite tune, and probably not the favorite of many bluegrass players, but it became its own thing. It kept going up the charts and it still won't die. There was a momentary influx of a tremendous amount of money but I was already making a lot of money in the studios.

I went back to doing studio work after the record came out and every time I'd walk in the studio all the guys would start playing that thing. I play with Tom Paxton quite a lot and he introduces me as Ned Beatty's stunt double. So it was fun. Not too many studio musicians have a hit record and this was almost a solo."

As coda to the story, Weissberg offers this anecdote: "A couple years ago, I was playing with Judy Collins down in Austin, and Ronny Cox was there. He told me how they actually filmed the scene to our music. The kid in the movie couldn't really play the banjo. He could move his picking hand fairly well but the left hand was a total disaster. Well, they found another kid, who actually *did* play and put this other kid on his knees, behind the chair, doing the fingering for the left hand. They shot it at such an angle that you couldn't tell. Ronnie described how they had one of the crew guys propping this kid up so he wouldn't fall off the porch. So that's what it is: one kid's right hand, and another kid's left hand. We had a big laugh over that."

§

Every aspect of it, for me, comes through the scientific method. I basically sat down with a pencil and paper and figured out what music is. Unlike a musician would, I did it by using intervals and numbers. I figured it all out mathematically before I knew there was anything called the Nashville Number System. I watch guys who can play jazz standards and just whip it out from inside their mind. I'm in awe of these kind of guys but I'm just naturally not that kind of person."

A high school chemistry teacher for seventeen years, Rick Aiello discovered the lap steel guitar in the mid 1980s while trying to woo a girl whose family owned a Ft. Lauderdale Polynesian restaurant that featured a Hawaiian band and floor show. To be nearer his object of infatuation, Rick bought a vintage Rickenbacher Silver Hawaiian lap steel and taught himself how to play it from scratch. He had never before played any kind of musical instrument. Though the relationship didn't work out, improbably, Rick landed a ten-year gig at the restaurant.

Fast forward to the 1990s when Rick and his physician wife, Chris, moved to Virginia where Chris established a family medical practice, Rick built their log home and the couple started having babies. Cooling his heels at home with the kids, Rick began to look for something to fill the time between diaper changes. Like Einstein working at the patent office, Rick had time to think. Through a combination of insatiable curiosity and dogged, stubborn persistence Rick discovered a lot of stuff about old lap steel guitars and pickups - things that people used to know but were lost to history as well as things that no one before him had ever bothered to investigate.

Rick probably knows more about vintage lap steel guitars and pickups and why they sound as they do than anybody on the planet. He has been the guy for innumerable steel players who thought their problem was insolvable before making Rick's acquaintance. I peeked through the door of "professor" Aiello's lab as we sat down to talk about vintage instruments, pickups, and his own line of cast aluminum steel guitars.

§

How did you start collecting vintage steels?

I only had three guitars when my wife graduated from medical school: a silver Hawaiian, a T-logo Bakelite, and a Jerry Byrd frypan. She said we can either go to Hawaii for a couple weeks or you can buy all the guitars you always wanted. I decided to buy the guitars. They weren't as expensive back then. I'd find something good on eBay and buy it. I had Richard Smith's Rickenbacher book and basically, I wanted one of everything he had in that book. That was my goal. I started buying things off eBay and I bought a couple that had bad pickups and that's how I got to know Jason Lollar (Seattle luthier and custom pickup guru). You gotta watch the pickups on vintage guitars. They're so fragile. There's one ground that comes out of the bottom and invariably, they're gonna bust so you've either got to learn how to fix them yourself or know somebody that can fix them.

You amassed a pretty good collection of Rickenbacher frypans and Bakelite steels and examined and measured them in great detail. What makes the Bakelites sound so good?

The best thing that Rickenbacher ever did was to have that integrated nut and bridge on the pre-war and wartime Bakelite models. That's where the tone is. And that's why a lot of folks don't like the postwars as much. It's not the size of the magnets – 1.5" versus 1.25" – that's irrelevant. I've checked enough of the bobbins and don't believe the windings changed significantly. They all come out in the 1.5 to 2.5 kilo-ohm range with #38 wire. So the difference in the sound that people go after and talk about so much is more from the integrated bridge than anything. That's where Rickenbacher made their big mistake.

How so?

I've seen enough of them now that I'm pretty convinced that all of the Bakelite bodies were molded before the war because on every one I've ever seen, if you take off the tailpiece, you'll see that the integrated bridge is filed off! They had the integrated bridge but just filed it off so they could put on that tailpiece. The fypans don't have that. The frypans have either a steel or bone insert. The bridge is built in but there's an insert that fits in there. When I decided to try and make my own steel guitar, that was the only thing that I to have. I didn't care about anything else. I had to have an integrated bridge and nut. You don't see that on any other guitars, at least I've never seen it.

How did you learn to cast repair knobs and repair Bakelite.

Everyone always wants those knobs. A lot of folks really care about their guitars looking authentic. So I had the representative knobs for all the guitars I owned. Basically, I made casts from RTV silicone - Room Temperature Vulcanizing silicone. You can make a mold for anything. I use polyester surfboard resin to cast the knobs. People like 'em. I've got a mold for the octagonal knobs. As for big Bakelite repairs, like large missing chunks, there ain't a whole lot you can do except mold-into the bakelite with black epoxy.

You've done a lot of scientific research on guitar pickups. Give me what role does size and magnet strength play in the overall sound and how does gauss and flux density affect a pickup?

To be general, there are a couple of ways to measure a magnet's strength. The most useful way is to measure its flux density which is a measurement of the lines of force per square centimeter. If you have a real strong magnet, there's going to be lots and lots and lots of these imaginary lines. It's a way of describing; they're like loops or rubber bands surrounding a magnet. Magnetic lines of force are a closed loop, like little rubber bands. They get stretched and where they curve would be the north and south pole of the magnet. The number of imaginary lines per unit area is the flux density and that's measured in gauss. It's like if you were hanging a weight off of one rubber band versus about 700 rubber bands. The more rubber bands or lines of force, the more powerful the magnet. Because it's a measurement of force per area, it doesn't take into consideration the magnet's size. So, you can compare magnets not by how they are but by how they are.

What types of magnets are most popular for guitar pickups?

A common electric guitar pickup, like on a Stratocaster®, uses alnico, or aluminum nickel cobalt, magnets. If you put a gauss meter probe on it, the average magnet would reach over one thousand gauss. This basically translates to a thousand lines per square centimeter. If you did the same thing with a neodymium iron boron magnet you'd get readings of 4-5 thousand gauss. So, alnico, even though it's used in just about every kind of pickup you see in electric guitars, is a weaker permanent magnet. It's one of the earliest permanent magnets made in the early 1930s. A lot of folks use ceramic magnets which are actually ferrite magnets and some people don't like them because they're generally stronger than alnico and they give what people perceive as a bright signal. What you're actually hearing is a greater signal-to-noise ratio.

How does one measure a pickup's gauss?

Well, you measure gauss with a gauss meter and gauss meters are pretty expensive. The big pickup makers have them. I found one that was somewhat reasonably priced. The way I measure everything, I put that probe dead square in the center. So if it was a horseshoe, I put the probe between the upper and lower flange, right at the mouth. A fully charged vintage Rickenbacher horseshoe with the cobalt steel magnets would read somewhere in the vicinity of about 200 gauss. They fluctuate depending on the grade of the steel used, particularly in the pre-wars. The steel that Rickenbacker used for their horseshoe pickups was 16% cobalt steel. It isn't manufactured anymore in any large quantities.

Does the gauss also affect the tone? Does higher gauss equal brighter tone?

Yes. The amount of information the pickup is sending to the amplifier is greatly enhanced by the stronger the field. Basically, what's happening is the more lines of force you have, the more disturbance of the field. To make a long story short, you're translating more information. The stronger the magnet, the more information and most of that information is in the upper register. So what you're hearing is higher bands that you never would normally even hear and people perceive that as brightness. It is, but it's not that the pickup is producing a super-bright sound; it's translating frequencies that normally wouldn't get translated.

Rickenbacher horseshoe pickups are generally considered one of the best-sounding pickups ever manufactured. How did you and Jason Lollar approach building reproduction horseshoes?

When I started prototyping horseshoe magnets for Jason, he was initially a little leery of using neodymium iron boron (NIB) magnets, but alnico is expensive now and they're having trouble finding it, and neodymium is being used all over the place in industry. I wondered why nobody was using' it for guitar pickups. One company was using NIB but just tiny, tiny little specs of it. Fishman Rare Earth pickups for acoustic guitars were using tiny specs of it. The alloys we were using to build our steel horseshoes, even after they were heat-treated, retained their magnetism but didn't charge up as high. People were saying, "These aren't as strong as the authentic Rickenbacher." So I said, "You want 'em strong? I'll make 'em strong!" I started messing around with designing a horseshoe pickup made of neodymium. I made about 50 prototypes and finally found a way to do it. It's a shame I can't make them anymore.

Why?

Rickenbacher hasn't put real horseshoe pickups on their guitars for years but they decided to trademark the design. A lot of bass players are apparently crazy over the Rickenbacher basses with horseshoe magnets and Jason thought we could sell a lot of them. He wanted to make a bass pickup line. I made a bunch of prototypes and they were all too strong. I eventually came up with one that I thought was pathetically weak but they loved it. I had to stop doing everything else because he was ordering so many of those bass magnets. I was spending all my time trying to keep up with the orders. We sold a bunch of those and apparently, Rickenbacher got hold of this and sent Jason a order. Supposedly, you can't trademark anything that has a function but Rickenbacher International filed for a federally registered design trademark and it made it through and passed in April, 2006. So it's now a registered trademark for Rickenbacher. As soon as that happened, we quit making them. I don't make magnets for Jason anymore and he shared enough information that I'm winding my own bobbins now. For the few guitars I make a year, I make everything.

What did you learn from making the horseshoes that you could apply to your own pickups?

As far as the design of my pickups, I like the magnetic field to surround the strings. That's what I feel really sets apart Rickenbacher guitars, the early Fenders trapezoid-shaped pickups and even the cheap Supro pickups. They all had magnetic fields that completely encompassed the strings. All the other conventional pickups have the flux coming up from just the bottom. It gives you better dynamics. If you pick hard, it sounds like you picked hard. If you pick soft, if sounds like you picked soft. The strings always vibrate in one plane but that plane rotates. No matter which way the strings vibrate they disturb the fieled that surrounds the strings more efficiently than a field that just comes up from underneath. I think you get a better response to the attack.

The early pedal steel guys tried upping the strength of the magnets but when you have that magnet just underneath the strings and you get too strong of a field it starts to pull the strings down and actually kills 'em.

It dampens their vibration. But when you've got the magnetic material 360 degrees around, you have equal and opposite forces pulling down and up. The forces that would normally dampen a string are canceled because they're equal and opposite forces. It's not a perfect cancellation but it still cancels it out to where I can build a pickup that's functional and has a magnet that's five times stronger than a Stratocaster® which translates to a signal that's gonna carry a lot more information. It's like comparing a telegraph signal to a fiber optic cable.

So that's what happened with our horseshoe magnets and then I started messing around with the design of the Fender trapezoid pickup and that evolved into my MRI pickups. I won't use anything else but them now. They're just so superior. Even if Rickenbacher hadn't basically shut us down I wouldn't put those horseshoes on any of my instruments anymore.

What's the advantage of the MRI?

It's that Leo Fender-design coil. Instead of having pole pieces, the coil itself surrounds the strings. In a trap pickup, you had not only the magnetic field surrounding the strings but the actual coil itself surrounded the strings. I was very interested in trying to come up with a reproduction trap but everything I tried just sounded, at best, exactly like a Fender . It didn't sound better. The traps have the magnets on either side and then they're yoked together by the steel top and bottom plates. So what's happening is the steel is acting like a conduit, allowing the lines of force to run through the steel. You get a field surrounding the strings but it's not equal. The bass strings are closer to that big magnet and then the treble strings are closer to the smaller magnet so the magnetic flux density changes as you go across the strings. That's why the Fender's were famous for such big bass tone and biting treble without a whole lot of mid range. They had that cool, scooped sound that some of us like so much.

And your MRI?

The MRI still retains that scooped sound – it's got a huge bass - but the flux density is even throughout the range. The middle strings are getting fed the same amount of juice as the outer strings. You have more mid range so it sounds a little bit closer to a horseshoe pickup than a Fender Trap, but essentially, you have the sonic qualities of both the trap and the horseshoe pickup.

Are pickups more microphonic as the gauss increases?

Yes. And that's another thing I battled, particularly with the horseshoe magnets. It's not really microphonic in the sense of a guitar pickup that you can put up to your mouth and talk into and that gets sent to the amp.
It's a vibrational thing. You can scream into these pickups and they're not gonna pick up your voice but you can take your fingernail and knock on the headstock of my first dustpans and you can hear it. So it's really more like vibraphonic, picking up vibrations.

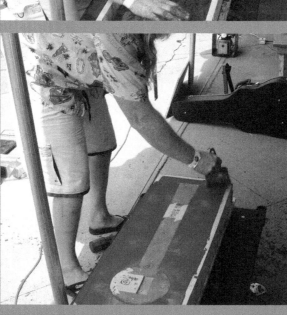

Some of the horseshoe magnets I made were like 800 gauss or four times stronger than a vintage shoe. I pick real gently so it didn't bother me at all. I thought it was glorious, but people that are heavy handed or used to playing acoustic instruments and hitting the strings hard, their attack was being picked up. So the higher the flux density, the greater chance you have of picking up ambient noise. That's one of the things that the MRI does much better than the horseshoes. They really cut down on the ambient noise.

On the last one I made, instead of using the normal way I secured the bobbin inside the magnet, I used a much denser material that helped damp out a lot of that vibration. The MRIs, simply because of the way they're built, in the way the bobbin is housed inside the magnet, helps cut down on some of that. Ever since I started putting MRIs on nobody comments on noise anymore. You can still hear a knock, but it's no more than on a Rickenbacher Bakelite or Frypan.

How did you first decide to cast your own steel guitars and what was involved in the process?

What led me to make my own guitars is that Jason Lollar was going to put out a line of lap steels that would feature our pickup but he had gotten so busy that kind of went on the back burner, and I wanted to get some steel guitars out there with our pickups. I'm not a very apt woodworker and I know there are cabinetmakers out there who are making very beautiful guitars and I couldn't come close to competing with those. Since I liked the frypans so much I looked into what was involved in sand casting. I knew I couldn't afford to die cast them. The more I read up on it the more I thought, "I can do this." So I purchased the equipment needed and the first couple that I cast were disastrous.

In what way?

I had tried the conventional system of sand casting with a top mold and a bottom mold and then those two molds are set together to form a three dimensional impression that the metal flows into and molds into. The problem was, at the size of the guitars I was building, each half of the mold weighed almost 200 lbs. So I had to take 400 lbs. and flip it over. I quickly learned that doing it the way professional sand casters would do it was out of the question. I decided to try a less conventional way by doing a half cast.

I decided I'd forgo any kind of details on the backside of the guitar and have the molded features I needed, like the integrated bridge and nut, on the front side of the guitar. So basically, what I have is a wooden which is a mock-up wooden guitar that I pack sand around. I use PetroBond sand, which is an oil-based sand. I started off trying to make my own as it's called in the trade and that was so time consuming that I opted to buy the professional grade oil sand. It's very expensive and comes in a 100 lb. box ready to use.

I put the mold down, the Mother, and pack the sand around it. It takes about an hour and a half to do. Then I flip that thing over, and pull the wooden mold out and pour the aluminum straight into the mold cavity.

I bought a furnace. My furnace will melt everything up to but including steel. The refractory material it's made of is only good to about 2600 degrees. So I can't melt steel but I can melt bronze and aluminum.

How hot does it have to get to melt aluminum?

The pouring temperature of aluminum is right around 1200 degrees Fahrenheit. I made a bronze frypan and the pouring temperature for bronze is about 2200 degrees Fahrenheit, almost a thousand degrees hotter. So you have to have it up past its melting point; hot enough so that it will go through the mold without seizing up or starting to solidify halfway through. It took me many, many tries to get the temperature right. It's very temperature dependent. I ultimately broke down and bought a high temperature pyrometer. It's like a thermometer for stuff that's that hot and that really helps. Once I got a uniform temperature that I could reproduce time and time again, I started making guitars that I didn't have to chop up and re-melt (laughs). It happened more often than I want to remember.

Did Rickenbacher cast their frypans?

What I believe from everything I've seen is that Rickenbacher frypans were die cast. There was a steel mold. I looked into getting one at the size of a Rickenbacher Academy model and it was about $65,000 to have the mold made. I said, "I'll stick with sand!" Adolph Rickenbacher was a master machinist and I believe he had the dies made, big giant steel molds. How they got the frypan necks hollow was a stroke of genius. They used an investment. It's sort of like a lost wax method. I believe they suspended a sand plug into that steel mold and would then force the molten aluminum in there. After it solidified, they pry those two halves of the mold apart and dig that sand investment out. That would leave a hollow chamber down the neck and into the pan. If you look carefully in the inside of any Rickenbacher frypan you'll see how it's all rough inside in that hollow chamber. You can see where the sand investment was. The Bakelites were also done with a steel mold.

Back to yours. What are the next steps?

It takes about 30-45 minutes to fully solidify and then about 4-5 hours to cool down enough so you can touch it. I set aside one day just to cast. I cast it and then set it aside. If you pull it out of the mold too soon, the aluminum will oxidize and form a thick layer of aluminum oxide, which is grayish and not very attractive. So if you let it cool in the sand itself the finish is much nicer and there's that much less work to do. Then you pry it out of the mold and the sand breaks up. Then you've got this ugly, big old chunk of aluminum shaped like a guitar.

On my first guitars, I included integrated frets but the aluminum would come into the mold with such force that I'd pour it into the pan and it would flow up the neck. It would bust up some of the higher frets, particularly around the twentieth fret area. I'd pour it but have imperfections in the 18, 19, 20th fret area. It sucked.

I'd have to chop that guitar up. I got tired of doing that so I ultimately went to casting a bare bones aluminum guitar with integrated nut and bridge and added the frets in myself like any luthier would. I use fret wire.

You've experimented with several different finishes as well as the classic Rickenbacher finish.

The black finish is done with a baked-on wrinkle paint like some of the earliest Rickenbacher frypans, in particular, the A-25s. I have a couple guitars and an amplifier from the 30s and they have this black wrinkle paint. I started off doing only the polished aluminum. I'd mill it down, do all the filing, and then sand with a belt sander. I'd move to a disc sander and then I'd go to hand sanding. That was taking a real long time to do and then I'd take to the buffer. I was looking for another kind of finish. People wanted color but the particular aluminum alloy I use for casting (A356) doesn't anodize well. Because of the silicone content, it leaves splotchy areas that don't get anodized to absorb the color. So unlike aircraft aluminum, which looks beautiful, this stuff doesn't anodize well.

I tried out all the commercially available wrinkle paints. Most of the ones you can buy at the auto store are used to paint valve covers. I didn't like any of them. None of them looked like the Rick finish. I was looking on the net and saw that Masserati Sports cars have their own wrinkle paint in red and black. I bought a quart for about $50 and it worked really nicely. I've been using that ever since. It has to be baked on for the wrinkles to come out even. I rigged up a system of heat lamps. I paint it then hang it from a log beam in my shop and blast it with the lamps for about 12 hours. Once it bakes on, it's real durable; a great finish. Everyone that's seen it and touched it really likes it too.

I've done guitars that are all polished, wrinkled fretboard and top and bottom not wrinkled and just the opposite: body and pan wrinkled and the fretboard polished and the last two I made for myself, I wrinkled everything (laughs). One is a 22.5" scale. We had just gone to see Pirates of the Caribbean so I named it the Black Pearl. For the sound you hear on those Andy Iona, Dick McIntire, and Sol Hoopii 78s, that sound is there in this guitar now and I can reproduce it every time with virtually no variation and that's a big thing.

Aesthetics are difficult to measure but you've made a career of applying scientific principles to art.

The type of science that I had always done in my non-musical life I've applied to music. Everything I've done, learning how to play the steel guitar, learning what music is, learning how to make magnets, improve the magnets, make different styles of magnets, making pickups and ultimately, learning how to build guitars is all science as far as I'm concerned. It's just my mindset. I look for as much information as I can find, I read all I can and then I think about it all day. When I was first trying to build a guitar, I thought about it all day – every day. It becomes all-consuming. It's classic scientific method. Learn everything that's been done before you and try to reproduce that and once you've reproduced it you try to better it.

Everything that I know about music I basically had to figure it out myself and I figured it out using the same kind of scientific principles and approaches that I've always used. There's a place for everybody and I just keep trying to find mine.

§

BILL ASHER

Sixteen years ago, when my first son was born, my wife at the time's best friend was friends with Billy. I didn't know him, but everyone around me knew Billy. He showed up at my wife's baby shower and he brought for my son the most extraordinary hand-made rattle you've ever seen; bird's eye maple, ebony, abalone. He engraved his initials in mother-of-pearl. That rattle took a beating, 'cause my oldest son could break bricks! It never cracked. To this day it's gorgeous. That was my introduction to Billy as a craftsman.

- Ben Harper

I first met Bill Asher ten years ago while I was writing a book about steel guitars. I'd noticed significant online scuttlebutt among steel players about a ground-breaking, solid body electric lap steel he'd designed for musician Ben Harper. When we spoke, I quickly realized that here was someone who was absolutely passionate about what he does. Whether riffing about tone chamber placement, pickups, finishes, or explaining the hoops he'd willingly jump through to please everyone from local players to demanding rock star clients, Asher was clearly a man of strong opinions but one who had his radar working overtime to understand exactly what musicians want and need from their instruments.

As I got to know him better, I learned that his years of repair experience, meticulous attention to detail, and solid understanding of what makes guitars sound good had made him the first-call repairman and builder for a slew of collectors, dealers, local musicians and world-class pros like Ben Harper, Jackson Browne, John Frusciante, Cindy Cashdollar, Robert Randolph, Colin Hay, Marc Ford and many more A-listers - people who wouldn't let their own mother even look at their vintage guitar's case, would happily entrust their axe to Bill.

As a kid, Bill Asher was drawn to the arts: painting, ceramics, and woodworking in particular, but as the son of Hollywood insiders, the world of lutherie might easily have lost him to an acting career. His father, [producer/ director] William Asher directed most of the classic episodes of I Love Lucy. His mother, Elizabeth Montgomery, was a beloved television icon for her role as Samantha, the witchcraft practicing housewife, on the 1960s sitcom, *Bewitched.*

As a teenager, Asher couldn't help noticing the lifestyle successful actors enjoyed and briefly considered following in their footsteps. "My mom discouraged me highly; I mean, intentional discouragement," he recalls. She said, "It's a difficult business, there's a lot of rejection and I think you should find something else that you want to do. If you're really absolutely passionate about it, go to drama school and become an actor, but I'm not going to help you." Chastened, the teenaged Asher returned to the wood shop and his obsession with guitars.

LEARN TO FIX 'EM BEFORE YOU BUILD 'EM

Like many Los Angeles teens in love with guitars, Asher started out jamming with friends and hanging at local hotspot Westwood Music where owner Fred Walecki regaled him with stories about Orville Gibson and Leo Fender. Bill says these talks helped him connect the dots between guitars as objects and the very human craftsmen who'd made them.

For his senior shop project in high school Asher built a Strat-inspired electric guitar. He showed the instrument to repairman Jeff Lunsford, one of the mainstays of the early '80s West LA guitar scene. Lunsford was impressed enough to offer Asher an apprenticeship that yielded him five years of invaluable experience in repairs, fretwork, guitar electronics, and learning the customer service skills that build a business. When Lunsford was offered the full-time opportunity to build Bob Dylan's home recording studio, Asher went to his parents for an $8,000 loan, bought Lunsford's tools, and at age 22, became a guitar shop owner.

"When I started out, I just wanted to be a guitar builder," explains Asher. "I feel lucky now that that didn't happen. I worked on repairs for 15 years before I built my first professional guitar. I'm really glad that I was here in LA where there's a great demand for repairs and working on really great vintage instruments. Working for pro players on nice guitars makes you take your work very seriously. There's no room for mistakes."

In the 1980s, more and more players were experimenting with modified electric guitars as builders mixed and matched electronics and intermingled the features of classic models in new ways. Asher was at the forefront of this trend and listened carefully to the players who came in asking for changes, such as putting a humbucking pickup in their Tele's bridge position for fatter tone, replacing a Tele neck with a Strat neck, or finding new ways to blend Fender twang with Gibson crunch.

"My first shop in the '80s was where I first met Jackson Browne. He walked into the store and I was like, "Whoa - Jackson Browne just walked in!" He hands me his Burgundy Mist Strat on which one of the pickups had died and asked if I could fix it. I said, "Well, these are the Schecter pickups that Obe uses in his guitars and I think I have a couple of old ones here." He got really excited that this young kid knew what he needed: "You *know* about these pickups?"

Jackson Browne picks up the story: "One of the things that we got straight right away when we first started to work together was that I didn't really care as much about cosmetic stuff. I'm interested in what guitars end up sounding like. I didn't care about aging the saddle so it looked like it was original. Having somebody work on your instruments to make 'em play or keep 'em playing is a serious thing if you've got 14 or 125 instruments you tour with. They've all got to work. I've spent more time with Billy then I've ever spent with any luthier, playing the guitars and thinking about what I want and like and for me, it's almost like having an in-house solution. I really kind of put myself in his hands. I don't know where I would be without him."

HOW ASHER JOINED THE A-LIST

"You really have to pay attention to what you're doing," says Asher. "Guys like Jackson Browne have a very particular way he wants a guitar set up and he's looking for a particular sound. It taught me to be very versatile in my approach to working on guitars. As a craftsman, you can kind of get into a groove of the way you think things should be done. I won't mention names, but we've had some guitar shops here in LA that were too opinionated and that was their downfall: "This is the way it has to be done and you don't know what you're talking about." I worked with pro players that I so respected and did [repairs] it the way they wanted to. It just took my skills to make it happen. That was a very valuable lesson for me."

Asher sold his first store in 1987, putting in stints with respected builders Rick Turner and Mark Lacey while gaining further experience in vintage restoration, repair, custom designs, sales and marketing. With Turner, Asher got the chance to work on instruments for high-profile bands and musicians like Fleetwood Mac, David Crosby, Steve Miller, Bonnie Raitt and T-Bone Burnett. "I was in the right place at the right time," he says. "Luckily, by the time I met Rick, I had the skills to run his repair department. I got introduced to a broader range of pro players and working on instruments for them at that level of quality honed my skills so well."

Asher eventually re-established his own shop in Santa Monica, continuing to learn from repairing many valuable vintage acoustic and electric guitar and experimenting with his own take on classic Fender and Gibson designs that, over time, evolved into his current line. Rather than slavishly copy classic designs, Asher took from each what he needed to realize his vision. "I think my guitars are aesthetically pleasing," he says. "I hear from players that the offset body has a very comfortable feel that brings the guitar closer to their body. They're initially drawn to the visual lines of the guitars and when they plug them into their rig, they're sold."

ORIGINAL DESIGNS

Asher electrics are know for their sustain and Bill feels the way he constructs his necks is a big contributor. "I've worked on a lot of vintage Strats and when I would try to remove those necks to adjust the truss rod sometimes the neck wouldn't come off," he explains. "You'd have to hit with the heel of your hand and sure enough, the

lacquer had over the years molded into each other." For Asher, the lesson was clear: "The more you can get the neck to meld into the body, the better. People lean toward Les Paul's and other glued-neck guitars as being a step above a bolt-on neck guitar but I think if you do the proper fitting and kind of meld the two pieces together with just a little bit of lacquer - that can be removable without too much trouble later on - I think you accomplish almost a set-neck transfer of tone into the body. People tell me that my Ultratone series [T-Deluxe, S-Customs, Marc Ford Model] definitely have a lot more sustain and more of a solid, glued neck vibe to them."

"For the headstock, I had to make a decision," he explains. "Even though I was making guitars that are patently influenced by Leo Fender, I really felt that the three-on-a side headstock design that Gibson stuck with – especially if you taper-in the headstock – would limit the break angle behind the nut. It added some stability for tuning, especially when using tremolo, and you can control the string angle behind the nut nicely at whatever headstock pitch you want." Asher's repair experience had also taught him that the area behind the nut was the place where headstocks tend to break. As a result, he uses an ebony faceplate on his headstocks to add mass, a volute behind the nut to reinforce the neck, and quartersawn woods to aid tone transfer into the body.

Bill's Telecaster-influenced T-Deluxe pays homage to its Fullerton California roots but takes some interesting side roads. His goal was to make a guitar for players who loved the simplicity of the Telecaster but wanted a different voicing with more tonal variety. "I didn't want to make clone guitars," he says. "If you want a great sounding, twangy Tele, you buy the Fender Telecaster. I didn't feel like I needed to make one of those. I was really excited about creating my own sound in that guitar with those two blade pickups and redesigning the neck pickup to be much more of a broadband sound with a lot more clear lows, nice treble and a little warmer, kind of honkier, bluesy tone out of the bridge pickup."

Guitarist Marc Ford sparked the idea for Asher's Stratocaster-influenced, double cut-a-way S-Custom guitars. "Marc approached me and said, "I just love playing a Stratocaster but I want the tone of my Les Paul Special," explains Asher. "Doing a mahogany body build with hand-wound P90s, I thought, would give him exactly what he was looking for for the Black Crowes tour in 2005." Asher views it as a honor to have the chance to collaborate in creating unique hybrid instruments that exactly suit a player's style and help them achieve their goals on stage and in the studio.

Jackson Browne is another fan of the S-Custom design. He owns several Ashers and recently ordered an alder model sporting a flamed maple top with trans-black finish and a pair of Tom Holmes humbuckers. As Browne puts it, "Bill's guitars work in a particular way, and I don't even know how to describe it, except to say the playability's amazing and the tone is incredible."

"We artists are always searching for various tones and sounds that will work and he really listens to the people that play. When something works, it's usually something you've found by accident, like a tuning you've found that sounds amazing. You hope that the thing will amplify well and if it doesn't, you have to keep working with it. In some cases we don't succeed with one pickup so we go on to another pickup and sometimes the project goes on for six months. Bill will stay with it; he's with you on the search."

Though he was initially somewhat unimpressed, Telecaster wizard Redd Volkaert is another convert to the Asher sound. As Asher recalls, "In 2009, I brought one of the first offset body Tele's that I did to Redds's concert at the Museum of Making Music, in Carlsbad, California. It had a P-90 in the neck and a stock Tele pickup in the bridge. He played it and said, "Bill, this is a pretty nicely made guitar but nothing I haven't seen before. It's cool, but not really for me." He was very blunt about that. Then I ran into him at the Arlington, Texas, show three years ago and my updated T-Deluxe caught his eye. He went, "Whoa, what is that?" He sat down and played it and flipped over the neck shape and tone." Volkaert loved the offset body and the feel of Asher's evolved guitar but he wanted more of the traditional Telecaster bite and twang. Asher responded with a prototype, he and Redd shook hands, and Asher now proudly offers a new Redd Volkaert signature model.

LAP STEEL GUITARS

Ben Harper is another seeker on the road to tonal karma. In Asher, he found the perfect partner. As Harper explains, "It's the perfect lap steel. Before I had the Asher I was any which way but loose, just looking and seeking from builder to builder. Certain things are made with little or no room for improvement and, like when Les Paul built the Les Paul or when Leo built the first Tele, Billy's lap steel is one of those special instruments."

It was guitar tech Bobby Carlos who first introduced Asher to vintage acoustic and electric lap steels. During down times in the shop, Carlos would point out the characteristics of various models and show Asher the rudiments of lap steel technique and tunings. So when Ben Harper called one day in 1998, Asher was ready. As he recalls, "Ben said, "I need something that's gonna give me more of an electric guitar's sustain on stage so I can really cut through a full band." Asher mulled it over and came up with a design that echoed the shape of Harper's trademark vintage Weissenborn acoustic guitars in a neck-through solid body design. For Asher's taste, many vintage steels were lacking in low-end response, so he designed his guitar to be larger and removed wood via cylindrical tone chambers – hollowed-out sections - that reduced weight and added back some of the airiness of the acoustic steels. He topped the mahogany body with a figured koa top and used a traditional Wessienborn-style bridge shape that was strung through the body. After sending the prototype to Harper, as Asher recalls, "Ben called me back a week later and said, "I need two more for the road. "How quick can you build them?"

Ben Harper remembers:
"Billy and I went through different generations until we finally hit the mark on it. Billy has a rare and deep command of both acoustics and electrics. He can bring out the acoustic nature of an electric and the electric nature of an acoustic. That's something that sets him apart. When we started designing the signature model, he

was able to incorporate hollow aspects of the Weissenborn into the solid maple cap signature model. I am as proud of that instrument as any song I've ever written. I'm not trying to take credit for something Billy made – it's Billy's brainchild - but he was kind enough to recognize I grew up in a music store, making and repairing instruments, so he utilized not only what I was looking for, but my understanding of what makes instruments tick. He let me be his co-pilot in the process."

Asher realized their steel design had wider potential and with Harper's blessing, he established it as the Electro Hawaiian Model. The production guitar sported the chambered mahogany body, koa top of the prototype with a set of Tom Anderson mini humbucking pickups (nicknamed Steelbuckers). The guitars were an instant hit with steel players and became renowned for their unique, cello-like tonal character.

Over time, Harper's signature model changed to reflect the intensity of his music with a design clearly influenced by Gibson's Les Paul. "He liked the feel and the design of that neck through body concept but needed something just a little bit more electric guitar-like and aggressive," explains Asher. "I built him that prototype back around 2000 and that's the prominent guitar he uses now. It's Les Paul-inspired as far as electronics and hardware. It's got a maple cap, Tone Pros Tune-O-Matic bridge and tuners plus two Seymour Duncan Custom Shop humbuckers. With this guitar, he gets much more of that classic, raw slide tone."

As Asher explains, "One of my big inspirations to come up with different models was I wanted lap steel players to have the same luxury of pickup, hardware and tone options as guitar players who have a plethora to choose from. I thought the lap steel was lacking that so that's why I keep designing the different models of steels. It's been very exciting for me to be one of the first guys to kind of re-invent the electric lap steel for modern guitar players. "Steel guitar guru Jerry Byrd advocated that a short, 22.5 inch scale was the ideal length for lap steel because the physics of that scale facilitate intonation and playability for his demanding slant bar technique. However, many pro players rarely use slants and Asher feels a 25" scale makes his instruments more approachable for a standard guitar player to be able to cross over to playing lap steel. "I think that what I'm doing with the longer scale and the multiple pickups and the larger body takes the lap steel to a more versatile place," he explains. "You can play any style of music on electric guitars on Gibson Les Paul or Fender scales, which are right around 25 inches - jazz, blues, rock, or country. I've been approached to make some short scale steels", he says, "and I did a couple custom ones but the short scale never really fit in with what I wanted to do."

Asher took the design to Asia for his Electro-Hawaiian Jr. line, a more affordable, off-the-shelf alternative to his custom models. "Hand-building guitars is a very time consuming and expensive venture, he explains. "It's a passion of mine that I love doing so I tried to build them in the shop and offer them at an affordable price but I still had to charge $1200 to $1400 to make it work. I wanted to open up a whole new audience of lap steel players so I realized I was gonna have to go to overseas production and spend a lot more money with the manufacturer to get the quality that I demand. That way, I could keep it around $799 retail to allow players to get a modern Asher lap steel at an affordable price. I think it's opened up the door for a lot of people who may not have had a chance to experience lap steel. We've built and shipped more than 500 of those now."

ACOUSTICS

After making meticulously accurate Weissenborn-influenced acoustic lap steels for several years, Asher's employee Jim Dugan suggested they build a Spanish-neck acoustic guitar that would commemorate Hermann Weissenborn's rare original. As Asher explains, "We took the Triple-0 body size and the color, scalloped the braces like a 1930s lightly braced acoustic and added the rope binding and a beautifully shaped 5-piece neck. It turned out to be magic."The first models went to former *Iggy Pop and the Stooges* guitarist James Williamson and singer/Songwriter Jillian Spear who took it straight into the studio. As Asher recalls, "The engineers were just blown away. We're now building these by custom order – about 10 a year – split between the commemorative Weissenborns [acoustic steels] and the flattop acoustics."

The shop's newest model, originally built for Colin Hay, is a round shoulder, spruced topped acoustic based on Gibson's Southern Jumbo sporting 40 year-old Brazilian rosewood for the back and sides. Asher's years of repair experience have given him a window into an instrument's future. "Thirty years from now it's gonna need a neck set but you don't want your rims or your bracing coming loose twenty or thirty years down the road," he explains. "That's why I use the more modern LMI glue for all the bracing and the structure of the guitar but we're using hide glue on our bridges and neck sets for tonal reasons. Hide glue is stable, gets nice and hard, and the tone transfer for hide glue is much better than the newer Titebonds 'cause they always maintain some elasticity which deadens and slows down the tone transfer."

NEW SHOP

Asher is now up and running at his new 1200 sq. ft. shop in Culver City. Four luthiers can work there simultaneously and Asher keeps it partially in the family with his brother helping out in the shop and wife Jessica handling the business side of things. While success has enabled him to step away from standard repairs Asher wants to keep his business from getting too large.

"I'm only doing vintage restoration by appointment or referral-only since we're focusing most of our energy on building," he says. "At this shop size, we can build about 100 guitars a year and that's feeling pretty comfortable for me at this point. I still have a great passion for vintage guitar restoration and it gives me a great connection to the players, so I want to maintain this small, exclusive shop where we build maybe 100 guitars a year and keep the demand there. That way I can still maintain my relationships with the LA-based artists. If I went to a factory model, it would be harder to keep up the personal side of my business."

It's the personal touch that has kept Jackson Browne a loyal Asher customer for more than 20 years. "He's a wonderful artist. He's really able to put himself at the service of another person's ideals. Nothing throws him and the stuff he makes is flawless in tone and playability."

As to the mysterious blend of craftsmanship, taste, Über-customer service, and Hollywood flash that goes into every Asher guitar, Ben Harper sums it up as well as anyone. "They're utilitarian; they're absolutely elegant and at the highest level of craftsmanship and artisanship. At a certain point, what's gonna separate these great builders from one another? Is a part of the essence of who they are in the tone, in the craftsmanship, and in the feel? Billy's soul is in the instruments. I know that may sound like a cliché but I tell you, his soul and spirit are in everything he builds."

§

CARROLL BENOIT

In an age of shoddy workmanship and corporate misdeeds, the phrase "traditional values" has become a catchphrase for marketing copywriters seeking to position their brand more attractively in the market. Character rarely tops the list of reasons to seek out an individual luthier but it's an interesting notion; can honesty, humility, and pride in workmanship help make a better musical instrument? Perhaps. In the small, Gulf Coast town of Mauriceville, Texas, Carroll Benoit, a man who embodies these values, is building some of the finest resonator guitars ever made.

In recalling his upbringing, Benoit says, "Everyone respected each other and a man's word was as good as gold, sealed by a handshake. We tipped our hats to show respect and removed them at the dinner table. I still hold on to those precious values." Benoit is a Cajun, descended from the French Arcadians exiled to southern Louisiana from Nova Scotia in the mid 1700s. Raised on a farm near Lafayette, his parents eked out a living as sharecroppers. As he recalls, "A share cropper kept one third of the crop and the owner got two thirds of it. Cotton sold for about $30 a bale and we were lucky to get three bales a year. We didn't need much money to live on because we raised our own vegetables, chickens, pigs and cattle. We never went hungry. Everyone spoke French and I didn't learn to speak English until I started school. Back then, if you spoke French on the school grounds the teachers would give you a whipping."

Benoit's father and brothers were master carpenters and instilled a work ethic that still guides him today. "My upbringing influenced me a lot in terms of building instruments. We were taught to do things right the first time and with lots of patience." This old school attitude is evident in Benoit's meticulous and flawless joinery, inlay work and the gleaming, high gloss finishes on his instruments.

Benoit found music at an early age, becoming part of a trio in his early teens. "The three of us had a little group and sang three-part harmony," he recalls. "We had a lot of fun with it and everywhere we'd go, we'd have a guitar with us. It was mostly country. I was brought up on Cajun music, but it was the thing you heard every day. We heard country music on the radio and liked it so that's what we played. I still gig on weekends with a small group at a local restaurant where I've been playing for the past 18 years."

Though he always played music as a sideline, Benoit and his wife Anita raised their five children thanks to his career as an electrician and builder of large, Las Vegas-style industrial signs. "We had to be skilled in working

with wood, metals, welding, electrical wiring, spray painting and whatever else was needed to do the job," he says.

While making signs for his day job, Benoit continued to build furniture and do carpentry as a hobby. Reading a copy of Woodworker Magazine one day in the late 1980s, he saw an advertisement for a Martin-style 000 guitar kit. Having owned and enjoyed Martins since he was a teenager, Benoit decided to order the kit. He successfully built the kit guitar and was hooked. "I was so amazed by the sound I got out of it that I just had to build another," he says.

Benoit began to build acoustic guitars from scratch, experimenting with various woods and body configurations. "After building a number of guitars I learned to get a very good sound out of them, so much so that I sold my Martin to a friend so I could buy better tools to make building guitars easier."

Then along came Eddie Ortego. Ortego is Benoit's friend and neighbor, a resonator guitarist and a disciple of the Josh Graves school of Dobro® playing. For two years, Ortego badgered Benoit to build him a resonator guitar. "He kept at it so long I got tired of listening to him," says Benoit with a laugh. Applying all he had learned from building acoustic guitars, Benoit caved in and built his first resophonic for Ortego. "I'm telling you, we were both amazed by the sound," he remembers. "I could not believe my ears. I had always liked the sound of the instrument, but after building this guitar I was overwhelmed by the tone I was getting, combining the acoustic guitar building methods with the resonator."

Benoit now has made 23 acoustic guitars, an acoustic bass, a violin, 4 electric guitars, and just recently, he surpassed the goal he'd set for himself of building 100 resonator guitars. He's crafted resophonics from traditional tonewoods, such as maple, walnut, koa, rosewood and spruce, as well as exotic woods such as zircote, zebrawood and macassar ebony. Benoit installs high quality cones spun by Paul Beard, and on some very special guitars, he's added stunning, gold engraved coverplates, tuners, and soundscreen frames.

Asked which woods are his favorites, Benoit replies, "Koa is a beautiful tonewood and hardwood. Koa was my favorite for a long time, and then I started experimenting with other woods. I've just built four guitars out of macassar ebony and everybody's flipping over them. They're really, really loving them. A couple had spruce tops; one had a maple top, and one was solid macassar top, sides and back," he explains. "I make more guitars with hardwood tops than spruce tops. They all have a different sound. Even with the same wood on different guitars they're gonna sound different."

Benoit takes special pride in having crafted several unique, one-of-a-kind instruments for clients. For New York player and collector, Howard Reinlieb, Benoit stepped way outside the resophonic tradition to help bring Reinlieb's ideas to fruition. Their collaborative oeuvre includes the Phoenix, a 7-string with flamed walnut back and sides, maple top, and redwood burl binding; and the Selmanator, a maple and walnut 8-string with the exact

body size of a Selmer Maccaferri Gypsy jazz guitar. Their masterpiece is probably the D'Benoito, a 9-string, archtop resophonic guitar inspired by the archtop jazz guitars of John D'Angelico. Its most unique feature among many is a wooden coverplate hand carved by a professional hat block maker.

In describing their unique collaboration Benoit says, "Howard is one of the most patient individuals that I have ever met. He basically knows what he wants in a guitar before he calls to order one. We've gone where no one else has gone in the resophonic world, and the rewards have been tremendous. On some of the guitars we really didn't know what kind of sound it would have. Howard understands that, and surprisingly every guitar I've made for him has had a unique sound."

Another unique instrument was built for a customer who was disabled, who has since died. As Benoit describes, "Because he had very limited mobility in his hands, he had a triangular pick fastened on a strap that he wrapped around his right hand and a 5" stainless steel bar that he strapped on his left hand. Understanding that he couldn't move very far left or right, we made it a short, 22 7/8" scale so he wouldn't have to move to get into position." Due to his disability, the man needed to play while almost laying down so Benoit put the position markers on the side of the fretboard and continued the frets on the side of the guitar so he could see them and also added a cutaway so he could reach up to the 15th fret without his hand hitting the side of the guitar.

"You don't see too many resonator guitars with a short scale," he says, "But man, the best sounding 8-string I've built was that guitar! It had more area in the back end and the screens were spaced a little differently. Because of the cutaway, one screen was a little lower than the other. It's such a rich sounding instrument." A former professional musician prior to his disability, the client was thrilled and inspired by the guitar to the degree that he returned to playing music after a twenty-year hiatus. Benoit in turn was inspired by his client's determination and tenacity. "He had a lot of guts to get out there and play. He hadn't given up on life."

In his regular models, Benoit also walks a different path than many current resonator guitar builders. "There are many great builders out there making very fine resonator guitars. I don't know if mine are any better, but they are different," he explains. "If you asked a hundred people for an opinion on this subject you'd probably get as many different answers. I have yet to build two guitars that sound exactly the same, even using the same type of wood. Most of my guitars have wood binding and purfling where many others use plastic. It gives my guitars a little more class, I think. You have to heat bend the wood binding. Plastic bends itself around the instrument. You don't have to heat it. I build only with solid woods – no laminates."

Competing with a banjo in a bluegrass band can be daunting for a resonator guitarist. Some builders have pursued designs that produce a bright, cutting tone, creating instruments sometimes described as a "banjo-killers" where increased volume is usually a trade off for diminished tone. Benoit follows a different muse where rich, mellow tone is the end goal.

According to Benoit, "I think it suits more styles of music or different styles than that bright sound. The tonewoods contribute as much to the sound of the instrument as the resonator does. What I mean by this is, if you build a guitar with laminated wood or metal you'll get a brighter, tinnier sound. Unlike these types of materials, solid tonewoods tend to soften the tone and give a nice, warm sound you can't get with the other materials. The hardwood naturally will give you a little brighter sound."

Benoit tops many of his guitars with spruce because he feels this mitigates the brightness and makes for a mellower sound than hardwood tops. "Even the all-hardwood won't be as bright as a laminated guitar," he says. "It just has a richer sound. I hope I don't upset too many carts. There are a lot of players out there that like the bright sound better and that's okay."

While many of the top resophonic builders, such as Tim Sheerhorn, moved to a post and sound baffle construction, Benoit stayed with the traditional soundwell design, adding his own modifications along the way. As he explains, "I prefer the soundwell method because I believe it plays a big part in the rigidity of the instrument at the point of stress. With a 10 1/2 diameter circle cut out of the top and also the pressure the strings contribute to this area, it needs extra strength. By tying the top to the back, so to speak, it keeps the instrument from buckling." In his view, the parallelogram openings on his soundwell design offer more area for the sound to travel through. "There's as much sound going through my guitars as you'd find using soundposts."

Now in his mid 70s, Benoit has no plans to expand his line beyond resophonic guitars; he's still captivated by its unique marriage of wood and metal. According to Benoit, "I've built other acoustic and electric instruments but none captivated me like the resonator guitar did - like it has for so many others. When you hear good players like Jim Heffernan, Mike Auldridge, Jerry Douglas, Rob Ickes, Eddie Ortego and others, you can feel their moods coming from the instrument. It's a wonderful feeling to know that I've been blessed to be able to build something that can be handed down to the next generation. I enjoy it tremendously. I'm addicted," he chuckles, "so I hope to continue as long as the old boy upstairs will let me."

§

For the last fifteen years, fretboard culture writers have been telling us that we're lucky to be enjoying a new golden age of lutherie. While traditional lutherie has climbed to its highest-ever pinnacle, a much different, underground folk art guitar culture has quietly flourished way, way under the radar. Rather than fine tonewoods, these builders use discarded gasoline cans for the bodies of their instruments and fashion necks from scratch or salvage them from standard guitars. For these luthiers, a lowly metal gas or oil can isn't just a utilitarian container used to fill a car or lawnmower's gas tank, it's a resonating cavity. For musicians in places like South Africa, Botswana and Namibia, there is simply no financial option to buy a factory made guitar but there are oil cans in abundance.

From Africa to blues-haunted Mississippi, to the California surf art scene and New Mexican lofts, "lug wrench luthiers" are re-imagining of what a guitar can be. Gas can instruments exist in a unique and intriguing universe unlike the rest of the plucked instrument world. What's perhaps most unexpected is the sublime sounds these instruments can offer. Fill 'er up!

GAS CAN GUITARS

ESTABAN BOJOURQUEZ

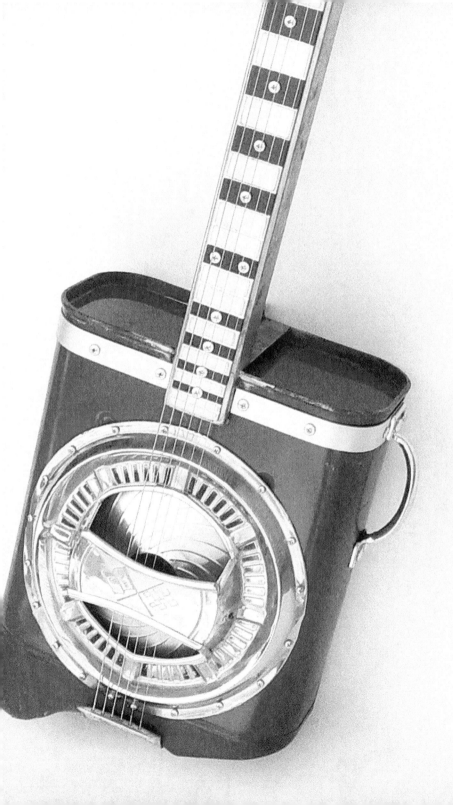

Estaban Bojourquez lives and works in Santa Fe, New Mexico. His gas can guitars transform found materials into beautiful expressions of playable art.

Bojourquez has worked as a sculptor and painter and it's through this fine arts lens that he conceptualizes and executes his one-of-a-kind instruments. These instruments celebrate the dings, dents and paint chips honestly earned by the material's original function but re-imagine them as new tools, useful once again.

§

SUPER CHIKAN

James "Super Chikan" Johnson is a musician, folk artist and guitar maker based in Clarksdale, Mississippi. His nickname stems from his childhood on the family farm and his fondness for poultry and his claim to understand the meaning of the noises they made. His friends and family soon began calling him "the old chicken boy" or "Chicken" for short. According to the *Mississippi Folk Life Folk Artist Directory*, "He received the other half of his moniker during a stint working as a taxi driver in Clarksdale. His speedy driving earned him the new nickname "Super Chikan."

Johnson acquired his first guitar (that had only two strings) from a Salvation Army store in Clarksdale. *Super Chikan* builds unique instruments using discarded gasoline cans that he decorates with paintings. In 1997, he released his debut album and since has been a prolific touring and recording artists performing at festivals around the world. Johnson's 2009 record *Chikadelic* received the 2010 Blues Music Award for best Traditional Blues Album. He has also received five Living Blues Critics Awards and the Mississippi Governor's Award for Excellence in the Arts.

BILL HARDIN

Although Bill Hardin now makes his living as a luthier, he was initially more interested in deconstructing guitars than constructing them. "I was always curious about how things worked - what was inside things - so in my teens, I took apart more guitars than I put together," explains Hardin, who builds guitars in Maui, Hawaii under the name of Bear Creek Guitars. The first time I realized you could build a guitar was when I got out of the Navy and I saw a class advertised at a community college. By then, I'd already taken apart three or four guitars and had a basic understanding of what was inside them. I got through that class at the community college in southern California, and I learned enough basically just to get my way in the door at Dobro. That's where I met Don Young."

Now co-owner of National Reso-phonic Guitars in San Luis Obispo, California, Young introduced Hardin to the world of resonator guitars, and more importantly, to the then mysterious Weissenborn-style Hawaiian steel guitar. "Don brought in this thing he'd made that he copied off some old original Weissenborn and it just blew my mind," Hardin says, "It was such a pure slide sound and just amazing." This unusual guitar with its flush frets and hollow neck, was designed to be played lap-style. It inspired Hardin to search out the old music that people would have played on it, and it sparked a desire to explore how these almost-forgotten instruments were constructed.

Before Hardin could really delve into the mysteries of hollowneck guitars, though, his budding career almost came to an abrupt end. One day in 1983, Bill Hardin was buffing an ornately engraved metal-bodied Dobro mandolin in preparation for plating. In a rush to get the job done, Hardin neglected to put the protective wooden cover over the well, the center cavity that holds the resonator. After a few seconds of pushing the mandolin against the buffing wheel, the instrument slipped, jamming his right hand into the spinning machine. With an odd mix of clarity, emotional detachment and a nearly hallucinogenic recall of the grisly details, Hardin remembers looking at his wrist bones starting to tear through the skin while two of his fingers dangled from his right palm, now attached solely by their veins. After turning off the buffer with his left hand, he screamed for help and then mercifully passed out as his colleagues used a hacksaw and tin snips to free him from the machine.

After several surgeries and extensive physical therapy, doctors told Hardin he'd recover only 50% of the use of his right hand and should consider a career change. He reluctantly took their advice and enrolled in a travel-

agent course to prepare for his new life. After only one mind-numbing day of class, he went home, pulled out a set of rosewood boards and started figuring out how to make a guitar again. Confounding expectations, Hardin regained the use of his hand and, one year later, Gabriella Lazar and Don Young offered him a chance to return to work. Two years later, he joined Richard Hoover at Santa Cruz Guitar Company.

Hardin describes his time at Santa Cruz as *a masters program in guitar making*. "It thrilled me. It frustrated me. If you're not getting frustrated now and then you're not trying," he says. "I was there 5 years and saw a really interesting time at SCGC. When I started there, there were 5 of us building guitars. The theory was for each person to try to build one guitar a week. The day I left Santa Cruz, the first CNC machines were on the way and I think they had 12 or 15 employees, all highly skilled luthiers and good guys out of Roberto Venn [School of Lutherie] and places like that."

Even as he constructed standard guitars at Santa Cruz, Hardin couldn't forget those early talks about Weissenborns with Don Young. He contacted Young, asking him what model of Hawaiian guitar might be best to use to launch his own lutherie business. "That was about the time Ben Harper was starting to record and it just seemed like the Weissenborn might be getting a new life. My idea was to get as far away from the Dreadnaught as I could get and the Weissenborn steel seemed to be perfect. I'd already chosen the name Bear Creek 'cause I lived just off a creek with that name. I ran an ad in *Acoustic Guitar Magazine* and started getting some interest, and it started taking off."

Hardin's days of hitting the swap meets and the flea markets in search of 25 or 50-dollar Hawaiian-style guitars began to pay off. He remembers finding quite a few at affordable prices, but they invariably needed repair. "The first one I took apart was an old Kona," Hardin recalls. "It was X-braced. It was what I would consider kind of a crudely made guitar but it had some pretty refined bracing in it for a steel string guitar – especially for its day in the 1920s."

Repairing old guitars also taught Hardin how Weissenborn had constructed their hollownecks. "There are certain things you won't know about them until you take them apart," he explains. "One of them was that they reinforced the whole neck with some kind of wood, usually spruce. You can't really see this by looking in the soundhole. The interiors were pretty crude, with saw marks and lots of glue dripping everywhere. And almost every brace in them was loose after all that time. Most of the ones I was picking up at flea markets and thrift stores were definitely beat up. So they were very crude, but they somehow held together."

The Hilos were ladder braced and there were some differences in the Weissenborn bracings in the early years, but by the mid 20s, they had a pretty refined X-brace with three struts coming off of it and a couple of transverse bars across the bottom, similar to what Martin uses. It was definitely a strong bracing pattern and it seemed to be the one to go with."

Anyone who has spent sometime around acoustic steel guitar players knows that they consider the original

Weissenborn instruments to have a special magic unduplicated by other instruments. Endless late-night arguments have raged over whether it's the quality of the koa wood, the body design, the rope binding, or simply their age that gives some of these instruments their unique, yet hard-to-define mojo. Hardin has little patience for metaphysical explanations.

"They weren't all great and they actually weren't all the same," he says. "You get some of the old Weissenborns that have a top that's maybe .150" thick or even more, and then you'll get one that's maybe .080" thick. And they really didn't select wood. It was whatever was running through the mill - some of it highly figured, some much less figured, and some with patches all over it. They all sounded different to me. Some of the magic of them is mainly the age - when you get a good one that has the original hide glue construction still intact and a shellac finish on it. The ones that sounded really great had all the original bracing intact. The neck angle also has a lot to do with how the guitars sound. The ones that I liked would usually have a little bit of a negative cant to the neck and fairly high action."

With his own line of hollownecks, Hardin looked for ways to improve on the original design. He reinforced the necks on his Bear Creek models and, gradually, found that increasing the thickness of the bracing and the top improved their tone. "I use a little bit thicker top than what someone would use on a standard Spanish or steel-string guitar," he explains. "With koa especially, if I get the top around .110" - about .030" more than I would do on a Spanish guitar – it gives me more sustain, more punch to the instrument. In the early days, I was maybe going a little thinner on my tops. If anything, I learned I like the koa a little fatter, especially for a steel-string guitar. It also gives the player a lot more versatility. They can play it in some higher tunings, with the strings at higher tension, without worrying about it."

One of the interesting cosmetic features of the early Weissenborns was the use of rope binding made of alternating light and dark shades of wood. Hardin is amused that some modern luthiers haven't yet figured out how to efficiently construct it.

"I've seen people put all the individual little pieces together," he explains. "I learned how to do it one day at Dobro by looking at a guitar that came in with some rope binding on it - I think it was actually Don [Young] and me sitting there - we were just looking at the guitar saying, "How would you do this? We came to the conclusion to lay it up in a big slab and then slice it off at 45 degrees into big strips. The thing I learned was that, without a backing on the binding, it was real difficult to work. Early in the Bear Creek days, I learned the trick of putting a little backing on the binding when you're sticking it on and then routing that off afterwards was the key. You could get some really intricate, small rope patterns without having to use the more chunky-looking rope."

Hardin feels the rope-bound guitars sound better but can't really explain why. "It could be the actual weight of the rope around guitar," he ventures. "They'll definitely take a hit. I've dropped guitars with rope binding and there will be a little smashed edge off the rope and maybe pieces falling off of the rope but the guitar itself won't be damaged. If I were to drop a guitar with solid rosewood binding, the body of the guitar would take the hit. A lot of the old rope bound guitars are missing pieces of rope here and there but it looks like the segmented binding protected the guitar."

The most visible proponent of Bear Creek instruments has been multi-instrumentalist, Bob Brozman. Brozman's endorsement helped put the company on the map and has extended to influencing Hardin's designs. As Brozman relates, "I have had and continually performed with Bill's instruments since 1997. His instruments are a big part of my sound and repertoire. A lot of my music would not be possible without Bear Creek instruments. I feel that they have gone beyond the Weissenborn in tone, projection, craftsmanship, joinery, and overall beauty."

"Bob's been a great promoter of my guitars and he's got a giant Weissenborn collection, which was really cool to see," Hardin says. "He's got real specific ideas of tone and usually, when I can meet those, it's pretty fulfilling. The guitar that I think Bob and I worked on that's the best was the little short scale kona that he tours with and he loves. I've actually made him two of them. What he does with that guitar pretty much blows my mind."

Brozman professes that curly koa delivers more sustain while straight-grained koa is louder but decays faster. Hardin believes the answer may have more to do with the thickness of the top.

"Koa is a pretty amazing wood for tonal characteristics," Hardin says, " but it varies a lot, with different densities from one board to the next. I can't say that the specific curl in the wood will give you a specific tone – especially with koa - because you can get some highly figured, really dense koa, and it will sound good if someone knows what to do with it and [you] thickenes it to the appropriate thickness and brace it right. I believe you can't really base a guitar on how beautiful the wood is but on how thick it is and what the luthier has done with it. I've also heard from other players out there that the plain koa's the stuff as far as what they want from the guitar.

"Bob may know some of this on a level I don't understand because he's got all these guitars he can compare right next to each other. I don't have 50 koa guitars I can swap at one time. I've seen curly koa that was amazing and I got great sustain out of it after building the guitar to the thickness that I prefer for the particular wood. I've been working with koa almost exclusively, and koa's getting more costly and kind of competitive to buy. It's becoming more and more popular and scarcer. It's only a matter of time. The large factories make beautiful guitars with koa, and they use up a lot of it."

Asked to explain the difference in tone between the Weissenborn hollownecks and the solidneck Konas, Hardin says, "The Kona has a little bit more of a guitar sound. It's got about the same volume as far as the chamber size, but it doesn't have the hollowneck - though some people call them 'semi-hollow' because it's hollow to the seventh fret. When I play an original Kona with a 25" scale it kind of sounds like you could be playing a Roy Smeck or an Oahu or another standard guitar on your lap. The Konas had a really nice bracing pattern so I think they're superior to some of the old student model Oahus, but it's a similar tone. I really like bottleneck style on a Kona. I think it sounds amazing. The first Kona I ever bought had four fishing lines as strings strung up like a

ukulele. Man, the fretwork in those things was just horrendous, so I'm sure if they were playable, they weren't a great Spanish guitar by any means.

I don't know why the Kona was produced. I think it might have been just to use smaller pieces of koa. The hollowneck is just its own animal. It's like the difference between a tricone and a single cone. It's got its own characteristics."

Hardin uses a 25" scale on his hollowneck instruments, unless a customer plans to use a high G tuning or wants to play it with lap steel tunings. He'll then shorten the scale so string tension won't overwhelm the instrument. The Kona guitars have a 23.5" scale - a 25" scale shortened by one fret. These guitars can accommodate higher tension tunings such as A, E, or C.

With an output now approaching 25 guitars a year, Hardin recently hired some help. "Milton Yamashita is working with me now," he explains. "He's an independent luthier and his company name is Kula guitars. He's working with me 20 hours a week doing gluing and carving braces but I'm down here seven days a week. I've been working with Milton for six or seven months now and we've managed to get a little ahead of the orders here and there. I finally had to take on my own finishing. I was actually even sending guitars to the mainland to get done for a while. It's also another whole job, in my opinion. The toxicity of it was annoying me but I built a spray booth here in the Maui shop and I'm doing my own high-gloss finishing and I also still offer a satin finish."

Hardin built ukuleles while working at Dobro and noticed there were collectors who would pay luthier-level prices for fine handmade instruments. Bear Creek makes two or three ukuleles a year, including a soprano model with a unique heart-shaped soundhole – a detail Hardin first saw on the soundhole of an old Gretsch that someone had customized. He debuted the heart-shaped soundhole at a guitar show in Healdsburg, California one year and it's continued to be popular with players.

Asked to name his own favorites, Hardin replies, "The baritones that Bob Brozman and I worked together on were really cool because we basically took the Weissenborn and we extended it all around inside by one inch. It came out to be this gigantic, kind of comical-looking Weissenborn and then when I strung that thing up, it just blew me away. It was like Weissenborn on steroids. I think the baritone was one of the coolest things because of the quick and immediate reaction from doing nothing but enlarging the guitar. I've also been working on a Hindustani slide guitar for a good ten years now. I'm just going through the wood selection now but I have all the drawings and the tunings down. I have decided to go with a carved top on it rather than a flat top, mainly because the luthiers in India seem to be coming out with an incredible sound out of theirs."

For the foreseeable future, Hardin plans to stick with the Hawaiian steel guitars that built his reputation but hopes to expand the line - in response to the economic pressures felt by every luthier working today. "It comes in waves but the economy's kind of choosing things right now; it's not necessarily the popularity of instruments," says Hardin. "I have noticed the Weissenborn isn't doing what it did five years ago but there's still steady interest. We're going to stick with hollowneck Weissenborn-style guitars and I am also adding parlor guitars.

I've got some really cool old small body guitars I'm working on. I don't think I'll ever go back to the Dreadnaught, but I'd like to explore resophonic guitars."

At my peak, I was about three years backlogged. Now, with Milton's help, I'd say we're getting down to about a year or so which gives me the luxury to think like this. Over the last ten years. I've just been building Weissenborns so it's exciting to consider some new designs."

§

STEVE SPODARYK

discovered Steve Spodaryk and his guitars at a guitar show. Walking amid the hedgerows of dreadnaughts, flamed-maple archtops and sound-ported paragons of modern lutherie, I spotted two guitars unlike any others at the show. Their six-on-a-side scroll headstocks, small body size and decorative appointments gave off a distinctly nineteenth century vibe. As I came closer, it was clear these were two of the most beautiful parlor-size instruments I'd ever seen. These guitars looked like museum pieces.

A luthier at a guitar show makes a unique compact with every perfect stranger who walks up and asks to play a guitar that may have taken months to build and may well be the lynchpin of that month's mortgage payment. Stepping into that bubble of trust, I asked Steve if I could play one of his guitars and gingerly carried it over to a corner. In that thickly carpeted hotel ballroom enveloped by the cacophony of voices, booming bluegrass, bossa nova and sensitive, make-me-cry fingerpicking, I was instantly impressed by the amount of sound coming from the little parlor guitar on my lap. Admiring the pearl and shell inlaid top, ice cream cone heel, and contrasting color inlays on the rear of the neck, I wondered what had possibly inspired Spodaryk to put so much obvious work into something as esoteric as a nineteenth century Viennese-style parlor guitar. I took Steve's card and resolved to learn more.

Like many builders, Steve Spodaryk spent much of his childhood in his dad's workshop. While he felt sure that he'd be building things from wood in some fashion throughout his life, his career took an initial detour. Spodaryk graduated from high school in 1984 at the start of the computer revolution and spent fifteen years in the corporate trenches building sophisticated software products. He viewed woodworking as an escape from the intense intellectual demands of his day job. Along the way, he discovered several writers, like James Krenov, who approached woodworking as an almost Zen-like lifestyle. Spodaryk was taking classes in furniture making with an eye toward a career change to cabinetmaking when fate intervened.

Spodaryk's neighbor visited him in his shop to play guitar and talk about woodworking. He encouraged Spodaryk to try building a guitar. "I thought, "that's crazy, nobody does that," recalls Spodaryk. "I'd never even heard of hand built guitars – this is the early '90s - but he had done all this research. He had the LMI catalog, he had the Cumpiano book and sources for wood and I became really interested in the whole notion of building a guitar."

After building several guitars Spodaryk learned that Massachusetts luthier Julius Borges was looking for an assistant. "I called him right away and kept pestering him until he said, "Okay, come out to the shop, bring a guitar and let's see what you're doing," he recalls. "We got along really well right from the onset. We stood next to one another for three years working side-by-side and that was my foray into building high-end instruments. Julius was building guitars that were very heavily influenced by the guitars of the golden era of Martin, the

1920s and 30s. That had been Julius' passion and it became mine too. Handling the old instruments and comparing them to the modern day equivalents, the factory instruments, it's like night and day," says Spodaryk. "To handle a vintage instrument and then to duplicate what you feel are its great qualities, that's the never-ending challenge. And then hopefully, you bring something new to it that's part of your personality and that suits you as a player and that other people might enjoy."

A lifelong history buff, Spodaryk became very interested in the very earliest Martin guitars, after reading Philip Bura's biography of C. F. Martin the 1st (C. F. Martin and His Guitars, 1796-1873, UNC press 2003). "These little guitars are largely kind of forgotten by the players of today and probably by many collectors too and I thought, maybe there's something about them that would be worth pursuing," Spodaryk explains. After three years with Borges, he made the decision to start his own lutherie business. "I didn't really know what I would find out. I was fascinated by the period details: the scroll headstock, the joinery, and the ice cream cone heel. I thought, here are some things that nobody is doing and haven't been done in quite a while. There's something about that hourglass shape and the short scale that might be different musically. I'm kind of dangerous when I let these ideas stew too long. Eventually they become reality."

As Spodaryk sees it, "Here's America as a fledgling nation; C.F. Martin comes from Europe with a particular kind of training and drops into the melting pot of New York City, and he takes all these influences from Germany, Austria, Italy and Spain and stirs them up with a big dose of Americana to produce the modern guitar as we know it. I'm passionate about it because I just think it's amazing; it's the story of America."

While built in America, the earliest Martin guitars retained many of the characteristics that C. F. Martin had learned in Vienna at Johann Stauffer's shop. Remarkably sophisticated for their time, Stauffer had patented the mechanical tuner prior to 1820, was using extruded fret wire, a cantilevered neck, ladder bracing, and mechanical neck joints that allowed instant, easy changes in an instrument's action. According to Spodaryk, "There are a lot of things about these guitars that have almost been forgotten for over a hundred years that builders are now coming back into. I thought there was something really cool and unique about these guitars. I still don't know if it makes any sense from a builder's perspective in terms of trying to make a living at it because I believe the market is extremely small for these instruments, but I felt like for my own journey as a builder, that this was a good place to start."

While Spodaryk admired the proportions and overall aesthetic of these parlor guitars, he didn't want to make a reproduction model with nylon strings but chose instead to use all he'd learned at Borges' elbow to craft a steel string instrument that would feel comfortable in the hands of a modern player. "The tops are X-braced and the backs are ladder braced," he explains. "Internally, they look like a Martin guitar from the 1930s. I've been using a very short scale on the smallest guitars: 24 inches, which is a scale that was used by C.F. Martin and by Stauffer. I'm also building a 24.9 Martin short scale, nominally a 25" scale. I've been scaling up the bodies a little bit so that they're more in line with a Martin size-1 or a Martin single-0. I may even do something a little bigger like a double-0, but I love the small-bodied guitars. To sit in your living room it's just so comfortable," he enthuses. "With the 25" scale length, the string tension is reduced, the fret spacing is more comfortable, and it's just really fun to play. The 1 3/4" nut, 20" radiused fingerboard and 2 3/8" bridge are the original dimensions, and I've left them unchanged."

Spodaryk's favorite top wood is Adirondack red spruce, a material he obtains, not from a lutheir's supply house, but from the source. "I harvested the wood up in Maine," he says. "I didn't drop the tree but I bought some logs at auction with a friend of mine. We took these trees and split them up into billets and then we re-sawed them into tops. I've been using those and they're really spectacular. I love European spruce too. I've got some beautiful Italian spruce. They're all a little different. The red spruce has kind of a bigger sound with more oomph to it and a lot of headroom. It can be pushed very hard." While Spodaryk's guitars won't be confused with a dreadnaught, they're not lacking in volume. "Part of the thrill of building these is because of the small size, they can really be built quite lightly without fear of an engineering failure," he says. "
The attack on these instruments is so fast because there's so little mass to get moving and the surface area of the tops is so much smaller, the bracing can be lighter and there's less string tension, so if you can hit all those variables just right, the guitars really sing."

One of the most striking features of the Stauffer Presentation Model was its ivory fretboard, which Spodaryk has managed to reproduce without violating today's import restrictions. He'd seen a modern Martin guitar with a white fingerboard and learned they'd used white Micarta, a synthetic material. "It's made from layers of fabric fused together with an epoxy," he explains, "and interestingly, it's almost identical in density to ebony. It took me a while to hunt down samples of the right size and color. The linen Micarta has a wonderful look that almost looks like ivory because it has a very faint grain pattern to it. It takes frets like magic, just sucks 'em right in and it's very wear resistant. Over time, as ebony becomes less available - and certainly the quality of ebony has dropped drastically in the last ten years - builders are going to be forced to consider alternate materials, like Micarta. I considered Holly and tried all kinds of light colored wood; I even tried bleaching wood but I just couldn't get anything that looked right until I found Micarta."

Examining the Spodaryk guitar at the guitar show, I noticed that its six-on-a-side tuners were mortised into a routed pocket in the back of the headstock. Additionally, the headstock had a metal backplate that conformed exactly to the headstock's shape. I asked Spodaryk the reasons for these details. "There's a loss of some mass and some thickness so the metal plate serves to tie that whole headstock structure back together," he explains. "It creates rigidity and adds a little bit of extra mass. The back plates [on the original Stauffer models] frequently had beautiful engraving done either freehand or with a decorative lathe. I've kept them plain because I honestly didn't know what people would want."

"The tuners were quite a challenge," he recalls. "I had talked to David Rogers in the UK who had actually been making a Stauffer set for a while but when I spoke to him, it wasn't something he wanted to continue doing. So I found some samples of old tuners and thought, "Well, I bet somebody could make these." I loved the Waverly tuners – that's all we used in Julius' shop. They're very light weight and everything about them is very high quality so they make a great platform for doing modifications. I started picturing them with changes: if I pulled them apart and then lengthened the shafts, I could do that staggered scroll headstock. If I cut the string posts down and re-turned the shafts, I could then mortise them into the headstock and if I took the base plates and machined those I could weld the tuners back together and make six-on-a-plate."

As Spodaryk recalls, "It was one of those projects where you could call a hundred machine shops and ninety-nine of them would just laugh and say, "I don't have time to do that" or "I don't want to deal with prototypes." But I found a machinist, Larry McMaster, who was right around the corner from me who said, "That's really interesting. I like doing prototypes." McMaster crafted a number of prototype tuners which he and Spodaryk used to refine the design. "Right now he's finishing a small run of ten sets for me that are just beautiful," says Spodaryk. That's a whole craft that I admire greatly because I know very little about metalworking where there's a lot of difficult lathe work. Larry just nailed it for me."

While the tuners are a unique and beautiful addition to his instruments, Spodaryk found they don't come cheap. "The downside is they're expensive to make," he acknowledges. "There are an awful lot of hours involved in each set of tuners but they're very distinctive and very functional and it's quite nice to have all six on one side, especially if you're a Fender player like I was. It's one of those things that is just very beautiful and elegant; more or less a violin scroll turned on its side."

Yet another eye-catching detail of Spodaryk's guitar is the alternating dark and light strips inlaid into the rear of the guitar's neck, a feature that often leaves even accomplished luthiers open mouthed. "It's really not that complicated," says Spodaryk. "It took me a long time standing around scratching my head and thinking, "How did they do this?" But once I had talked to Dick Boak at Martin I realized, "Of course! It had to be strips wrapped around a core. It's a throwback to the early 19th century and actually quite a bit of fun. It's a lot of handwork. I get to pull out my best planes and thickness those strips and taper them all, and then cooper them like a barrel so that they can be wrapped around that concave shape. The light strips are made from a synthetic white fiber product that Michael Gurian sells. It works really nicely with hand tools."

As he researched the construction details of the original presentation model Stauffer Martin guitars Spodaryk wondered how they'd created the half-circular inlays that surrounded the guitar's top. "My feeling was that they were button blanks originally," he says. "C. F. Martin likely went down the street to one of the tailors in lower Manhattan and took button blanks and cut them in half. The people at Martin told me, "Oh yeah, we found a whole box of these button blanks back at the old mill." You just look at it and say, "How could they do this?" Yet all it required was to drill a whole in a piece of plywood with a router bit of the right size

and bushing and just make it work. Sometimes those things that look really complicated have a simple solution."

Spodaryk's obsession with period-perfect detail extends to building his own custom cases. "I think it's one of these moments where I've lost my senses," laughs Spodaryk. "I couldn't find a case to fit these small-body guitars and I learned that Martin had often made cases in the shop when they had some down time using mahogany, walnut and poplar. I'm using walnut and I've made a few out of poplar, painted black like the originals."

Spodaryk's current models include the Presentation Model, named more for its level of ornamentation than body size, as well as other more modestly appointed Stauffer-inspired parlor guitars that still retain pre-Civil War details like the scroll headstock and ice cream cone heel. Though he acknowledges that the work required to add these details to his instruments increases their cost, Spodaryk doesn't want to build guitars solely aimed at collectors. "I'm the first to admit that they're expensive and I wish I could produce them more cheaply, but I think many people appreciate the amount of work that's gone into it and feel like they're actually a good value for what they're receiving," he says. "I'm constantly fighting the urge to go bigger to try to be a little more mainstream about this, do things that would appeal to a wider range of players but I'm going to stick with these small-bodied, European-influenced parlor guitars for the foreseeable future.

I'm part of a group of people trying to uncover some of the mystery around these really early Martins and I think there will be more scholarship and more attention drawn to these guitars and that will only help what I'm trying to do. I've learned it's hard to do something different but I don't have to make a thousand people happy. If I can make six or eight people happy I can call it making a living. If I could make ten people happy a year, I would be overjoyed."

§

TIKI BAR GUITAR

According to Tiki historian, Sven Kirsten, "*The wish to forsake the benefits of civilization for a simpler, natural lifestyle is as old as "civilization" itself. .…The fair climate, natural beauty, passionate natives, and abundant resources of exotic foods seemed to promise an existence free of the restraints and stresses created by the cultured communities of the Western world.*"

Exotic, rum-laden tropical drinks couldn't hurt either, thought Ernest Beaumont-Gantt - better known as Don The Beachcomber - who opened a small Hollywood bar in 1934 that tapped into a nationwide obsession with the Polynesia of the imagination.

The roots of this fascination with Tiki culture stem from the yearlong Panama Pacific International Exposition held in San Francisco in 1915, which first introduced Hawaiian music and culture to the mainland. This "first contact" spawned a four-decade fixation on the music and culture of the South Pacific. Hollywood and Tin Pan Alley fueled the public's imagination by providing a steady stream of tropical-themed songs, films, and literature that made strumming a ukulele, surrounded by beautiful native girls and soft island breezes seem much more appealing than punching a time clock.

James Michener's novels, Thor Heyerdahl's 1947 sea voyage on Kon-Tiki, and the nostalgia of G.I.s who'd served in the islands during WWII all served to catalyze Polynesian pop culture and bring it to full flower by the late 1950s. For several generations of Americans, this Pacific Rim mélange of ersatz Hawaiian, Tahitian, Maori, Micronesian, and Samoan culture promised a temporary escape to a hip, exciting fantasy world. For guitarists, steel guitarists, bassists, and ukulele players, from approximately the mid-1920s through the mid-1960s, it promised a regular, rent-paying gig.

From its origins in chants and native percussion, island music seemed to absorb just about any genre with which it rubbed shoulders, from the hymns of the missionaries to German military marches, ragtime, hot jazz, Tin Pan Alley hokum, big band, and Andrews Sister-type harmony vocals. By the 1930s, Hawaiian music had been largely commercialized into a musical stew known in the Hawaiian musical community as Hapa Haole, or "half white" music. Most often, the music was played by some combination of archtop rhythm guitars, rhythm ukulele, upright bass, and electric steel guitar.

Hawaiian-born steel guitarist Ralph Kolsiana had a long career in the swank supper clubs and Tiki restaurants of southern California including Club Zamboanga, The Seven Seas, Don The Beachcomber's and other long-gone Pu Pu temples like The Tahiti Hut, Chi Chi Club, The Waikiki, The Hawaiian Gardens, and Disneyland's Tahitian Lounge. Kolsiana's steel guitar style married sweet island melodies with Hot Club-style swing. He even had something of a side career carving stone Tikis and providing Polynesian-themed decorations to restaurants.

Ralph Kolsiana's progression through a series of instruments mirrored that of many Tiki musicians. Starting as a beginner on an acoustic guitar with a nut extender, a device for raising the strings off the fretboard for lap-style playing, Kolsiana played Rickenbacher frypans and Bakelite models, Nationals, and lastly, a Fender Dual Professional.

In contrast to scuffling for jazz gigs, chasing the tail of the self-destructive comet of rock stardom, or working round the clock in the studios, competent musicians could enjoy the equivalent of a day job. Many American cities had Polynesian restaurants that offered live music. In Chicago, Beau Sterling played a steady gig at the Chicago Marriott's Kona Kai restaurant for years. "My sister was a hula dancer and that kinda steered me into this Polynesian thing," he says. "I was still in my teens when I started working with some of the local groups in the Chicago area. I played a National double-neck steel and rhythm guitar and sang. You have to like the music. A lot of people said they didn't like it at first, but boy, after a while it really grows on you." A typical Kona Kai show included Hawaiian standard tunes like Little Grass Shack, Blue Hawaii, and Beyond the Reef, interspersed with exciting performances by the fire and knife dancers.

In Florida, steel guitarist Dick Sanft had an even longer standing gig at Walt Disney World, spending 20 years at their Tradewinds restaurant. According to Sanft, "You played anything and everything … Hawaiian, pop, people's requests. We were paid scale by the musicians union. I started in Phoenix at a hotel called Samoan Village back in the 60s, stayed there for 5 years, then traveled to wherever the job was. When Disney world needed a steel guitarist, I came to Florida."

As the sound of the Telecaster, Stratocaster, and Les Paul became the dominant voices of a new youth culture, the Tiki restaurants and their fabricated pop cultural mythology gradually became a dusty, unhip corner of the musical universe. Now, with time and perspective, Tiki music is cool again and resonates in the music of modern surf bands like the Los Angeles-based *Blue Hawaiians*, San Francisco's *Smokin' Menehunes*, and Florida's *Haole Kats*.

§

PHOTO CREDITS

Despite an exhaustive search, we have been unable to locate the copyright owners of some of the photographs in this book. Therefore, we have proceeded on the assumption that no formal copyright claims have been filed on these works. If we have inadvertently published a previously copyrighted photograph without permission, we advise the copyright owner(s) to contact us so that we may give credit in future editions.

Cover Illustration: Andy Volk. Shutterstock, Veer, Personal images.
2 & 5   Illustration: Andy Volk. Veer, Personal images.
6   Muriel Anderson courtesy, of Muriel Anderson, Photo: Rusty Russell.
10   Muriel Anderson & Les Paul courtesy of Muriel Anderson. Photo: Chris Lenz.
13   Muriel Anderson courtesy of Muriel Anderson. Photo: Chuck Winans.
16   George & wife, Evelyn Barnes 1975 courtesy of Alexandra Barnes Leh.
19   George Barnes courtesy of Alexandra Barnes Leh.
21   George Barnes & Art Ryerson, Armonk, NY 1968 courtesy of Alexandra Barnes Leh.
25   George Barnes & Bucky Pizzarelli courtesy of Alexandra Barnes Leh.
27   George Barnes, *Music in Velvet* TV show 1948 courtesy of Alexandra Barnes Leh.
28   Gino Bordin courtesy of Les Cook.
31   Gino Bordin courtesy of Gerrit Venema.
32   Jerry Byrd. Photomontage courtesy of Mike Ihde.
34   Cindy Cashdollar courtesy of Cindy Cashdollar. Photo: Dale Haussner.
37   Cindy Cashdollar courtesy of Cindy Cashdollar. Photo: Dale Haussner.
38   Amos Garret. Photo: Trudie Lee. Courtesy of Trudie Lee.
41   Amos Garrett courtesy of Amos Garrett.
44   Ben Harper, Esquire Magazine, Nov. 1999. Courtesy of Ralph Loren/Esquire.
47   Courtesy of Bill Asher
48-52   Courtesy of John Montelone
55   Bud Isaacs courtesy of Jody Carver.
56   Slowly 45 rpm courtesy of Ron Middlebrook.
56   Sho-Bud advertisement. Bud Isaacs RCA cover courtesy of Ron Middlebrook.
57   Mexican Toy Guitars. Veer Images.
58   Ray Jackson courtesy of Ray Jackson.
61   Ray Jackson courtesy of Ray Jackson.
63   Nancy Hamilton. Library of Congress.
64   Illustration: Andy Volk. Photo courtesy of Nato Lima.
68   Nato Lima & Guy Van Duser courtesy of Nato Lima.
69   Nato Lima with guitars courtesy of Nato Lima.
71   Nato & Michiko Lima courtesy of Nato Lima.
72   Illustration: Andy Volk. Tony Mottola, 1960s Gibson Guitar advertisement.
74   Joaquin Murphey courtesy of Jody Carver. Photo: Jody Carver.
77   Joaquin Murphey courtesy of Michael Johnstone.
79   Girl with guitar. Veer Images.
80   Skip Pitts courtesy of Charles Pitts/The Bo-Keys.
82   Illustration: Andy Volk from a photo courtesy of Paul Marossy.
83   Guitarist. Veer Images.
84   Elliott Randall courtesy of Elliott Randall.
87   Elliott Randall courtesy of Elliott Randall.
88   Louie Shelton courtesy of Louie Shelton.
91   Illustration: Andy Volk. Photo: Library of Congress.
92   Johnny Smith courtesy of Lin Flanagan
94   Johnny Smith courtesy of Lin Flanagan

95   Johnny Smith courtesy of Lin Flanagan
97   Johnny Smith courtesy of Lin Flanagan
98   Johnny Smith and Arthur Godfrey courtesy of Lin Flanagan
99   Child musicians. Oahu collection. Photo courtesy of Gerald Ross.
100   Gabor Szabo. Frame grab from Hungarian performance film.
102   Gabor Szabo. Illustration, Andy Volk from photo by Fortepan/ Zoltán Szalay.
103   Barney Isaacs and George Kuo courtesy of Dancing Cat Records.
104   Bill Tapia on stage courtesy of Bill Tapia.
106   Bill Tapia with band 1930s courtesy of Bill Tapia.
107   Bill Tapia with uke courtesy of Bill Tapia.
108   Eric Weissberg courtesy of Eric Weissberg.
112   New Dimensions in Banjo & Bluegrass. Record Cover.
113   Soldier/Guitarist in Viet Nam. National Archives/Illustration, Andy Volk.
114   Rick Aiello courtesy of Rick Aiello.
120   Photo Montage. Photos courtesy of Rick Aiello.
122   Cast steel guitar photo courtesy of Rick Aiello.
127   Bill Asher shop photo courtesy of Bill Asher
130   Asher T-Deluxe & Marc Ford Model bodies courtesy of Bill Asher.
133   Asher Ben Harper Lap Steel Headstock courtesy of Bill Asher.
134   Asher Hollow-T with Bolivian rosewood top.
137   Asher Elctro-Hawaiian Model 1 with custom pinstriping.
138   Steinar Gregertsen w/ Asher lap steel courtesy of the late Steinar Gregertsen.
141   Carroll Benoit shop photo courtesy Carroll Benoit.
143   Resophonic interior courtesy of Carroll Benoit.
145   Macassar Rosewood resophonic courtesy of Carroll Benoit.
147   Howard Reinlieb with his Benoit guitars courtesy of Howard Reinlieb.
148   Texaco Station. Provenance unknown.
149   Estaban Bojourquez courtesy of Esteban Bojourquez.
150   Road Warrior gas can guitarcourtesy of Esteban Bojourquez.
151   Resonator gas can guitar close-up courtesy of Esteban Bojourquez.
152   Portrait courtesy of James "Super Chikan" Johnson.
153   Gas can guitar courtesy of James "Super Chikan" Johnson.
154   Gas can bass guitar courtesy of James "Super Chikan" Johnson.
155   African American guitarist, late 1960s, illinois. Library of Congress.
157   Bill Hardin & Doug Degenhart, Volcano Guitar Works. Courtesy of Bill Hardin.
163   Bear Creek lap steel courtesy of Bill Hardin.
165   Spodaryk guitar courtesy of Steve Spodaryk.
166   Front: Spodaryk guitar courtesy of Steve Spodaryk.
169   Rear: Spodaryk guitar courtesy of Steve Spodaryk.
170   Detail: Spodaryk guitar courtesy of Steve Spodaryk.
171   Spodaryk portrait courtesy of Steve Spodaryk. Photo: Bob "Yukon" Stubblebine.
153   Guitar heel detail: Spodaryk guitar courtesy of Steve Spodaryk.
172   Illustration: Andy Volk. Photo courtesty of the late Ralph Kolsiana.
174   1940s *Don The Beachcomber* menu courtesy of Kevin Bullat.
176   Steel guitarist Beryl Harrell & band. Steel Guitar Forum.
179   Andy Volk & Ed Gerhard courtesy of The Music Emporium, Lexington, MA.

ACKNOWLEDGEMENTS

Thank you to String Letter Publishing (Cindy Cashdollar) and The Fretboard Journal (Muriel Anderson, Gino Bordin, Ray Jackson, Nato Lima, Skip Pitts, Bill Asher, Bill Hardin, Steve Spodaryk & Tiki Bar Guitar) for their kind permission to allow me to include material here that first appeared in their pages. Special thanks to: Sarah Ahlgren, Bill Asher, Cindy Cashdollar, Bill Hardin and Mike Neer as well as all the great musicians and luthiers who were so generous with their time. Joaquin Murphey article originally published in Joaquin Murphey: Classic Western Swing Steel Guitar Solos by John McGann & Andy Volk, 2004. Kenneth Rainey's excellent article, 'Steelman Extraordinaire', Vol. 22.1/The Journal of Country Music, was a significant resource for content and quotes for this essay as well as the Seattle Western Swing Music Society, allmusicguide.com, Michael Johnstone, Chas Smith, Jody Carver, and public domain posts on www.steelguitarforum.com.

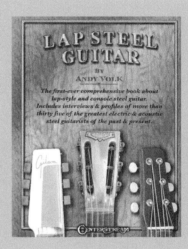

Andy Volk's book *Slide Rules* is available from the author: volkmediabooks.com. *Lap Steel Guitar* is available from the from centerstream-usa.com or Amozon.com.

End Page: The author giving a talk and demonstration about lap steel tunings along with guitarist Ed Gerhard and luthier Bill Asher at The Music Emporium, Lexington, Massachusetts.